I0212724

PRAISE FOR *WHAT IS ECUMENISM?*

"Antoine Arjakovsky's unique experience with practical ecumenical engagement in various cultural and geographical contexts, particularly those of Eastern Christianity, shines through in his book. Drawing on the remarkable breadth of his theological and philosophical knowledge, he calls for a profound rethinking of the idea of ecumenism by shifting the paradigm from the traditional, limited understanding to an 'ecumenical metaphysics' that aims to provide comprehensive spiritual insight into the contemporary world and guidance for a better future."

—**YURY P. AVVAKUMOV**, Archbishop Demetrios Associate Professor of Byzantine Theology, University of Notre Dame

"In his book *What is Ecumenism?* Antoine Arjakovsky revisits the concept of ecumenism in light of the latest theological and philosophical ideas. His stimulating interdisciplinary reflection invites readers to reconsider the movement towards unity in light of a true 'ecumenical metaphysics'—ecumenism as the unity of all in all, and not merely as the unity of Christians. An insightful book offering valuable perspectives on the most recent developments in the ecumenical movement."

—**HYACINTHE DESTIVELLE OP**, Œcumenicum, Angelicum, Rome

"In this seminal essay on ecumenical metaphysics, Arjakovsky provides a masterful review of decades of literature, theological reflections, historical narratives, philosophy, and much more, to share the foundation of a 'new understanding of reality, of a new epistemology, both trans-disciplinary and trans-confessional but also trans-religious and trans-convictional.' To this end he draws on the spiritual and metaphysical traditions of the East and West, associating the Western openness to transcendence with the Eastern 'sense of harmony,' thereby presenting a new epistemology concerned with all experiences that lead to the unification of consciousness, from Zoroastrianism to Christianity, from Shamanism to Taoism. Arjakovsky invites the reader to discover that older searches for theological and practical Christian unity, if and when allowing for challenges and renewal by an emerging ecumenical metaphysics, enable a revisioning of environmental stewardship and peacebuilding, critical to the survival of future generations."

—**AZZA KARAM**, President and CEO, Lead Integrity

"Drawing from the well of extensive experience in ecumenical practices and reflection, Antoine Arjakovsky argues here for an ecumenical metaphysics: a search for a knowledge of reality that is dynamic, open, tensive, and in active dialogue with a range of Christian voices together with Buddhists, Muslims, Jews, Hindus, scientists, peacemakers, philosophers, and others. Set against a contemporary horizon characterized by violent conflict, religious and confessional rigidity, systemic inequality, human rights abuses, and ecological disaster, Arjakovsky moves across history and disciplines to develop an ecumenical metaphysics as a sapiential compass both personal and universal, participatory and collaborative, to help us think through the challenging problems of our age."

—**LISA RADAKOVICH HOLSBERG**, Department of Theology, Fordham University

"The quest for unity in our fractured world is an urgent necessity. Between the naive belief that divisions are secondary and the fundamentalist defense of ossified identities, we need a rational basis for fruitful dialogue. Antoine Arjakovsky's book can serve as a starting point for such conversation about how to bridge the divides between people, nations, and religions."

—**ZDZISŁAW SZMAŃDA OP**, Director, Saint Thomas Aquinas Institute, Kyiv

WHAT IS ECUMENISM?

What is Ecumenism?

A Metaphysical Vision

ANTOINE ARJAKOVSKY

Foreword by Odair Pedroso Mateus
Translated by Penelope Cavill

Angelico Press

First published in French as
Qu'est-ce que l'œcuménisme?
© Les Éditions du Cerf, 2022
© Angelico Press, 2025

All rights reserved:
No part of this book may be reproduced or transmitted,
in any form or by any means, without permission

For information, address:
Angelico Press, Ltd.
169 Monitor St.
Brooklyn, NY 11222
www.angelicopress.com

ppr 979-8-89280-154-6
cloth 979-8-89280-155-3

Book and cover design
by Michael Schrauzer

CONTENTS

FOREWORD

WHAT is at stake when we use the term "ecumenism"?

For some it is a refusal to conform with the abnormal situation of confessing One Church and living among churches that refuse each other the sacrament called "communion." For others, it describes the coming together of Christians and churches in active counter-cultural opposition to contemporary megatrends that threaten life on earth, particularly the life of the most vulnerable. Others see in the term "ecumenism" a non-normative description of the infinite diversity of Christianities emerging constantly from declining Eurocentric Christianities.

Introductions to ecumenism or overall presentations of the ecumenical movement often reflect the variety of answers given to the question of what is at stake in the term "ecumenism."

An introduction to ecumenism that dedicates its initial chapters to the rifts opposing Eastern and Western churches, or Reformation churches and the Roman Catholic Church, and goes on to review the progress accomplished by the dialogue among them, is virtually confining the term "ecumenism" to the problem of the relationship between the One Church confessed in the Creed and the many churches experienced in history.

An introduction to the ecumenical movement that approaches it in the wider context of the human struggles for liberation presupposes that in the term "ecumenism," the overcoming of what separates human beings in their diversity is inseparable from the overcoming of what divided Christian churches in the past.

For Antoine Arjakovsky, however, there is much more than all that at stake when we use the term "ecumenism."

Against the background of the contemporary climate disaster, catalysed by the Industrial Revolution as a powerful expression of modern, secularized rationality, and against the churches' "conceptualist and confessional rationality" that underscore, according to him, their search for visible unity through convergence in ecclesiology — as in *The Church: Towards a Common Vision* — Arjakovsky brings to light that "much more" by arguing for an "ecumenical metaphysics."

What does he mean by it? Ecumenical metaphysics, he writes, is "the foundation of a new understanding of reality, of a new epistemology, both trans-disciplinary and trans-confessional but also trans-religious and trans-convictional...." It may release Christian ecumenical studies "from the often narrow approach of confessional ecclesiologies." Churches, he notes, "tend to reduce the universality of the Church to their own conceptions of the universal, which often leads to contradictory positions."

The Central Committee of the World Council of Churches was once required to clarify the sense in which the WCC used the term "ecumenical." Its official answer, in nineteen words, includes the word "whole" no less than three times: "It is important to insist that the word "ecumenical," wrote the Central Committee, is properly used to describe "everything that relates to the whole task of the whole church to bring the gospel to the whole world." It could have used "whole" four times, had it written "the whole gospel," a timely reminder in today's flourishing Christianities.

Along the same lines, the outstanding German ecumenist Ernst Lange would later use the term "household" — which, in the Greek *oikos,* is at the root of words such as ecology, economy, and ecumenism — to describe the challenge of the ecumenical utopia. "The Christian conscience," wrote the author of the classical *Die ökumenische Utopie,* "has to learn to adjust itself to the larger household to which it was from the very beginning directed, namely to the household of the whole inhabited earth. It has to be trained in a new sensibility, a new awareness of the world and time, or, rather in its own most original and basic sensibility."

Later on, the former general secretary of the World Council of Churches, Konrad Raiser, in *Ecumenism in Transition*, a fundamental contribution to the debate on the "crisis" of the ecumenical movement, would build on Lange's visionary insights by contending that instead of a crisis, the ecumenical movement is transitioning towards a new self-understanding, a new paradigm in which the search for Christian unity is inspired, renewed, indeed subsumed by the Christian and non-Christian stewardship of the "one household of life."

In a similar effort, Arjakovsky's *What is Ecumenism?*[1] invites the reader to discover that the apparently old-fashioned theological and practical search for Christian unity may in fact appear in a new and timely light if it allows itself to be challenged and renewed by an emerging ecumenical metaphysics in which what is at stake concerns our salvation and therefore our survival, and that of future generations.

Odair Pedroso Mateus
Director of the Commission on Faith and Order
of the World Council of Churches (2015–2022)

---

[1] Antoine Arjakovsky, *Qu'est-ce que l'œcuménisme?* (Paris: Cerf, 2022).

INTRODUCTION

ECUMENISM is something I have been practicing for at least four decades. I started my journey in the early 1980s as an ecumenical representative for ACER-MJO (Action chrétienne des étudiants russes—Mouvement de jeunesse orthodoxe), a youth movement to which I belonged as an Orthodox Christian. This opportunity allowed me to meet Christians who fought, in Europe and the rest of the world, for greater justice, for peace, and the care for creation within the World Council of Churches (WCC),[1] the World Student Christian Federation, and the Ecumenical Youth Council in Europe. My marriage to a Roman Catholic was a source of infinite joy and wonder, but also of an awareness of the existing gap between the institutional logic of churches and the prophetic reality of the small churches created by mixed couples.

When I became director of the French University College of Moscow in 1994, I was privileged to meet eminent spiritual and intellectual figures of different religious denominations, such as Father Alexander Men, or Elena Bonner, who had fought against communist and antireligious ideology. Subsequently, in 2004, I also had the privilege of founding with friends an Institute of Ecumenical Studies in Lviv within the Catholic University of Ukraine.[2] At a time when Ukraine seemed irrevocably divided between its East and West, the Institute of Ecumenical Studies mobilized in favour of the possible unity of the Ukrainian nation on the basis of its Christian and European heritage, both multi-confessional and multi-cultural. With friends from different Christian

---

[1] https://www.oikoumene.org (last accessed August 5, 2025).
[2] http://www.ecumenicalstudies.org.ua/eng/about-us (last accessed August 5, 2025).

denominations, we also founded the Ukrainian Christian
Academic Society and the Ukrainian Ecumenical Social
Weeks. These structures have provided a basis for reflection, but also for the peaceful commitment of Christians
to the dignity of every human being, and for democracy,
during the revolutions that took place in Ukraine between
2004 and 2014. During this time, I continued to participate in the activities of the WCC, particularly in the
reflections of the Faith and Order Commission, and by
attending the 2006 General Assembly in Porto Alegre,
Brazil. Later, I had the opportunity to teach ecumenical
science in Paris at the Collège des Bernardins[3] and the
Institut Chrétiens d'Orient,[4] to publish articles in ecumenical journals, to participate in several inter-faith and
inter-denominational seminars, such as those of the Fra-
ternité d'Abraham or the Community of Sant'Egidio, and
to organize conferences on ecumenical themes as diverse
as the Radical Orthodoxy movement or the history of the
Council of Florence.[5] It was a period rich in encounters
with the most distinguished contemporary theologians
from John Milbank to Cardinal Walter Kasper, from
Elisabeth Behr-Sigel to Konrad Raiser.

In parallel to this existential and ecclesial commitment,
I had the opportunity to write a doctoral thesis on the
history of Russian intellectuals who emigrated to the West
after 1917.[6] The ecumenical dimension of their thought

---

[3] https://www.collegedesbernardins.fr/intervenant/antoine-arja-
kovsky (last accessed August 5, 2025).

[4] https://www.institutchretiensdorient.org/blog/l-actu-de-l-institut-
1/l-ico-un-vrai-besoin-dans-le-monde-francophone-4 (last accessed
August 5, 2025).

[5] A. Arjakovsky and B. Hallensleben, *The Council of Florence (1438/39)–
an Ecumenical Rereading* (Fribourg: Aschendorff, 2020); Adrian
Pabst and Christoph Schneider, eds., *Encounter Between Eastern
Orthodoxy and Radical Orthodoxy: Transfiguring the World Through
the Word* (Ashgate, 2009).

[6] Antoine Arjakovsky, *The Way, Religious Thinkers of the Russian
Emigration in Paris and Their Journal, 1925–1940*, trans. Jerry Ryan,

and their political, social and ecclesial commitment were at the heart of my research. Indeed, these religious thinkers, for the most part Orthodox Christians, were the main initiators of the ecumenical movement among Eastern Christians, such as Father Sergei Bulgakov, the co-founder of the Fellowship of St Alban and St Sergius in 1928, Father George Florovsky, one of the founding members of the World Council of Churches in 1948, and Mother Maria Skobtsova, the initiator of Orthodox Action, an association which opened a new page in the relationship between Christians and Jews in the Russian world. In the course of this research, and, later, within the framework of the Association of Christian Philosophers, of which I became president, I have had the privilege of meeting and exchanging ideas with many contemporary philosophers who take the question of faith and reason to heart, from Paul Ricoeur to Catherine Pickstock, from François Jullien to Abdennour Bidar, from Christos Yannaras to Jean-Marc Ferry.[7]

I remind the reader of these few personal milestones to explain that the fivefold dimension of the "ecumenical movement," at once civilizational, political, eschatological, interconfessional and metaphysical, is not foreign to me. I would add that this ecumenical journey has helped me to understand that the act of knowledge cannot be the fruit of the process of objectification alone; it necessarily implies the phenomenon of subjectivation. This is why ecumenical metaphysics does not lead only to a science of ecumenism. In an even more fascinating way, it also offers an ecumenical grasp of science.

---

ed. John A. Jillions and Michael Plekon, foreword by Rowan Williams (Notre Dame University Press, 2013).

[7] See, for one example, the debate with J.-M. Ferry in May 2021 at the Collège des Bernardins: "Le temps est-il venu de réhabiliter la métaphysique?," Collège des Bernardins, https://www.youtube.com/watch?v=uX4xLoWhpM8 (last accessed August 5, 2025).

This is probably the reason why, after forty years of commitment, teaching and research, I have sought to make a contribution to the ecumenical movement by renewing its intellectual and spiritual foundations. Indeed, the gap between the vibrant reality of the ecumenical movement and the ignorance of which it is the victim has become glaring. Worse still, the phenomenon of fundamentalist violence has developed over the past twenty years with the increase of secularization. As Adrien Candiard has shown, the banishment of God found in fanaticism only retains, from faith, the commandments it reveals; it is the counterpart of idol worship, widespread in secularized societies which, from faith, take only the freedom it allows.[8]

All over the world, the crisis of ultraliberalism, but also the advent of dictatorial regimes, have brought to light a systemic crisis combining anti-ecological economic development and the creation of unprecedented social injustices due to their media coverage. It is becoming increasingly apparent that the States and their cultural elites are less and less able to propose an ideology to take the place of religious traditions, as has been the case in the West since the time of Enlightenment. At the same time, the West has experienced a staggering decrease in priestly vocations, and a growing disaffection of the laity from the traditional structures of the Churches. It also becomes clear that the modern conception of the Church, both the vertical and confessional, but also its postmodern, horizontal, adogmatic and individualistic outgrowth, are no longer able to meet the expectations of people increasingly frustrated at not being able to be heard in their quest for meaning, truth, universality and fellowship.

The thesis I recently developed in my *Essai de métaphysique œcuménique*[9] captures the ecumenical movement not

[8] A. Candiard, *Du fanatisme, quand la religion est malade* (Paris: Éd. du Cerf, 2020).

[9] Antoine Arjakovsky, *Essai de métaphysique œcuménique* (Paris: Éd.

only as a civilizational and political phenomenon, as an intra-Christian and inter-institutional reality, but also as a metaphysics in its own right. Presented in summary form in this essay, the latter is ecumenical primarily through its principles and methods. It conceives the universal as a personal reality, grasps being as a sapiential, polar, eschatological reality, and is based on a ternary logic, inclusive and transdisciplinary. Centred on consciousness, at once divine, cosmic and human, it strives, through the art of dialogue, interpretation, narrative and creativity, to distinguish the different levels of consciousness according to the dual relationship, vertical and horizontal, that living beings maintain with respect to reality. This approach provides an escape from the confrontation between those who believe in heaven and those who do not. It provides a new framework, in tension with the relationship between faith and reason, that includes all the different religious and convictional systems. By proposing an original epistemology, ecumenical metaphysics makes it possible to offer a new framework for new ecumenical practices, from peace-building to environmental protection. It gives new horizons to ancient professions, that of the educator and that of the artist.

This non-exhaustive introduction nevertheless presents the heart of this new discipline of ecumenical metaphysics that I am deeply convinced will be called to develop and to bring illumination in the coming years.

du Cerf, 2021). For an English translation, see Antoine Arjakovsky, *Towards an Ecumenical Metaphysics* (Brooklyn, NY : Angelico Press, 2022). https://www.christianunity.va/content/unitacristiani/en.html.

I

The Five Meanings of Ecumenism

ECUMENISM is associated in the collective consciousness with the movement of rapprochement among the various Christian confessions. Little-known to the general public, as it is not mentioned in most school curricula or in the mass media, this movement affects over 2.4 billion people worldwide. Indeed, Christians represent a third of the global population, estimated at 7.5 billion by 2020. In today's globalized and highly connected world, interactions between Christians of different denominations have become, for the most part, an everyday reality, visible or invisible, conscious or unconscious.

In fact, considerably more people are engaged in ecumenism, since the movement of rapprochement between Catholic, Protestant, Anglican, Evangelical, Pentecostal, Orthodox, Syriac, and Coptic Christians has had an impact on the relations of the Christian world with the Jewish, Muslim, Hindu, Buddhist, and Confucian worlds. As stated by the Catholic theologian Yves Congar, the Church is both the Christian community, the body of the faithful, and the institution of salvation founded by Jesus Christ, which in this instance concerns all humanity "since Abel," that is, since the origins of humanity. This is the reason why the Dicastery for Promoting Christian Unity,[1] based at the Vatican in Rome, has a specific commission dedicated to relations with the Jews. It also cooperates closely with the Dicastery for Interreligious Dialogue.[2]

---

[1] https://www.christianunity.va/content/unitacristiani/en.html (last accessed August 5, 2025).

[2] https://www.dicasteryinterreligious.va (last accessed August 5, 2025).

This shows that ecumenism goes beyond the framework
of interfaith relations alone. More generally, the ecumenical movement sees itself as a worldwide movement, with
a body of doctrine and administrative structures for all
people everywhere. This is why the World Council of
Churches has symbolically located its headquarters opposite the United Nations building in Geneva.

Some images, often ephemeral, succeed in reaching
the collective consciousness. For instance, in Jerusalem
in 1964, when Pope Paul VI and Patriarch Athenagoras
embraced each other; or in Assisi in 1986, when the main
religious leaders of the world gathered around Pope John
Paul II to pray and reflect together. The more mature
amongst us remember the *aggiornamento* movement of the
Catholic Church at the time of Vatican II in 1962–1965,
and the promise of the Council Fathers, since repeated by
all subsequent Roman pontiffs, of their irrevocable commitment to the reconciliation of Churches and ecclesial
communities. In the Eastern Churches of Istanbul, Moscow, and Bucharest, as well as those of Damascus, Cairo
or Kerala, despite the — often tenacious — conservatism,
it was recognized that the ecumenical movement should
be distinguished from the colonial policy of Western
states, as was often the case during the last millennium.
Although, again, there is no total consensus, Christians of
the Protestant tradition, in Uppsala as in Lagos and San
Francisco, are well aware of how much their Churches
and communities played a decisive role in the foundation
of the World Council of Churches in 1948 in Amsterdam, or in the historic rapprochement with the Catholic
Church at the end of the twentieth century, to the point
of reaching an understanding with her in 1999 over the
justification issue, which was the primary source of con-
tention leading to the dissolution of the Church's unity
in the sixteenth century. From now on, both Protestants
and Catholics agree that all people can be justified before

God by faith in Jesus Christ, and by cooperation in God's saving work in the world.

This movement of interfaith and interreligious encounter has had decisive political consequences. The role of Catholics and Protestants in the founding of the European Economic Community in 1957 in Rome, the commitment of both Protestants and Orthodox in the Conference of European Churches to tear down the Berlin Wall in November 1989, or the reconciliation of Christians in Northern Ireland during the Good Friday Agreement in Belfast, April 10, 1998, are all examples of the many significant impacts of the ecumenical movement on the political life of nations and international relations for at least half a century.

Ecumenism, however, as its name suggests, is a broader and older phenomenon. Before being an interdenominational and political movement, it is a worldview like idealism or materialism, a personal and at the same time communal way of considering the world and its destiny. Its originality, compared to modern ideologies, resides in the desire to think together about the universal and the personal, the true and the beautiful, the unique and the different. Modernity was marked not only by the division of Christian denominations, or their failure to maintain unity and diversity, as was the case with Catholics, Protestants, and Orthodox following the failures of the councils of Basel and Florence at the end of the thirteenth century, but also by a schism between faith and reason. As a result, realities that were previously perceived as transcendent, meta-historical, and possessing common properties such as truth and beauty, goodness, and justice, become increasingly disjointed in the consciousness. The evolutions of European art, from Romanesque to Gothic, Baroque to modern, testify to this progressive dissociation of what was formerly described as transcendental. This is why contemporary ecumenical action-thinking does not seek only to heal the wounds of the spiritual body that humans form together, thereby transcending the old limits of confessional identities. It proposes a new kind of universalism, philo-sophical in the sense that it understands the being in all its sophianic depth, and theo-logical in the sense that it sees human dignity as a manifestation of the divine character of the person. Against the dissociations of the modern and post-modern eras, *oikoumene* denotes, at a certain level of consciousness, the space-time that unites the universal with the personal, as well as the natural and cultural. In this perspective, the environment is not considered as a mechanical reality, but as the infinitely complex interrelation of the worlds proper to all kinds of subjects, for each of which reality is never an abstract universal datum, but a singular medium, which never ceases to build itself correlatively to these subjects themselves.

Let us take the example of environmental science to underline the metaphysical, and thus spiritual, foundations of such a conception of *oikoumene*. Mesological thinking,[3] brilliantly developed by the Japanese philosopher Watsuji Tetsuro, has made it possible, with the concept of "mediance," to think about the dynamic coupling of every human being, of any society, with its eco-techno-symbolical milieu.[4] Ecumenical metaphysics incorporates Japanese Zen Buddhism's representation of emptiness, but it deepens it through a sapiential idea of mediation capable of combining cultural and natural realities in distinction. For, according to the ecumenical worldview, the world is not only a relational space-time; it is also a created reality, or, to put it another way, an offered reality. It has a

---

[3] Mesology, or ecological science, studies, in an interdisciplinary and transdisciplinary way, the relationship of living beings in general, or human beings in particular, to their living environment. See A. Berque, *Écoumène, introduction à l'étude des milieux humains* (Paris: Belin, 2000).

[4] *Purifying Zen, Watsuji Tetsurō's Shamon Dōgen* (Honolulu: Hawaii Press, 2011).

consciousness called to become personalized. Persons are microcosms, confronted with an uncreated reality, a non-objectifiable reality permeating every concept that presents itself in and by itself. In a certain way, each time one jointly considers unity and diversity, the true and the beautiful, the good and the just, it is a question of ecumenism. This is why the ecumenical worldview cannot belong to a single Church or religion or confessional tradition. Fundamentally, it is a very early metaphysics, predating all divisions, anchored in the inaugural event of the covenant offered by God to human beings. It is also radically new, because it is concerned to a greater extent with the authentic meaning of history, the advent of the Kingdom of God on earth, as announced in the last book of the Bible.

Let us take a second example of meta-confessional ecumenism, this time drawing on pop culture, to dispel any possible preconceptions about ecumenism. It was a matter of ecumenism when, in 1985, a group of American artists got together to form the band "U.S.A. for Africa" under the musical leadership of Quincy Jones to record the song "We Are the World" in support of the famine victims in Ethiopia. Michael Jackson, Lionel Richie, Bob Dylan, Bruce Springsteen, Stevie Wonder, Tina Turner, Cyndi Lauper and many other American singers decided to unite around these simple words:

> There comes a time
> When we heed a certain call
> When the world must come together as one

> There are people dying
> Oh, and it's time to lend a hand to life
> The greatest gift of all

> We can't go on
> Pretending day-by-day
> That someone, somewhere soon make a change

> We're all a part of God's great big family
> And the truth, you know, love is all we need

We are the world
We are the children
We are the ones who make a
brighter day, so let's start giving

This song undoubtedly had a global impact because it inspired Bob Geldof to organize the double Live Aid concerts in Philadelphia and London that same year. Broadcast by the media, these concerts were watched by more than two billion people. Versions of the song have been produced for Ethiopia in other languages, in France, for example, by the group Chanteurs sans Frontières, with the participation of popular artists such as Renaud, Michel Berger, Véronique Sanson and Jean-Jacques Goldmann. A new English-language version, updated by the Covid crisis in 2020, was also performed and released by Lionel Richie and Katy Perry.

The current growth dilemma of the ecumenical movement, public ignorance of it, and growing disaffection among Christians themselves can be partially attributed to the disconnect between a narrowly religious understanding of it and a movement for greater fraternity and solidarity with all people. For, in an age of globalization and fundamentalist resurgences, even taking into account the reality of existing disagreements among Christians, it is difficult not to see that the common faith in a triune God and in the resurrected Christ that unites Catholics, Protestants, and Orthodox according to their diversity is infinitely greater than what divides them. Now this simple observation should prevent any form of fearful, close-minded and exclusive attitude. Most of the Churches recognize today — admittedly *mezza voce* for some — that they do not yet in themselves reflect the pleroma, the Kingdom of God on earth, that they are partly responsible for their divisions, and that they must constantly renew themselves in order to be able to prepare for the advent of divine-humanity.

Despite this humbler attitude, most of these religious institutions, hostages to a conceptualist and confessional rationality they have helped to forge, demand, as at the WCC assembly in Busan in 2013, the recognition of a "visible unity" by all and in all places in a homogeneous and verified way, before allowing the faithful to commune together with God.[5] However, the evangelists insisted on the fact that one must believe in order to see, and not the other way around. Moreover, the most competent theologians recognize that the sacrament of Communion is a sign of visible unity, but also that it is a source of invisible grace capable of overcoming the artificial divisions of this world.[6]

Thanks to great ecumenical figures such as Thomas Merton, the American Cistercian and Trappist monk, or Tenzin Gyatso, the fourteenth Tibetan Dalai Lama, the complementarities between the theocentric and sophiocentric religious systems have become more evident. How, then, in spite of the many original initiatives for a more convivial world, such as those of André Chouraqui or Hans Küng, can Christians continue to live in parallel worlds with other religious traditions, and always postpone the common effort for "unity in truth"? How can these Churches, if they want to be faithful to their evangelical convictions, and thus be credible, continue to try to pull out the speck that they see in the eye of other faith traditions without first recognizing the plank that clouds their own eyes?

Many Christians ask themselves these questions and do not find convincing answers in the statements and attitudes of their ecclesial institutions. This has accelerated the now massive phenomenon of belief without belonging,

---

[5] *L'Église, Vers une vision commune*, document Foi et constitution, no. 214 (Lyon: Unité chrétienne, Fédération protestante de France, 2014), vii; https://www.oikoumene.org/sites/default/files/Document/The_Church_Towards_a_common_vision.pdf (last accessed August 5, 2025).

[6] G.-H. Ruyssen, *Eucharistie et œcuménisme* (Paris: Éd. du Cerf, 2008).

of clerical stiffening of some Christian institutions, and, in reaction, of anti-religious secularization (and vice versa). In reality, the "ecumenical winter" that specialists have been talking about for more than thirty years is the result of a widespread ignorance of the semantic evolution of the very notion of ecumenism. Yet this complex process (since several meanings of the same term can coexist in a potential or actual way) testifies to a profound evolution of consciousness. This could lead, provided we grasp the whole depth and all the implications, to an extraordinary paradigm shift, the double exit of humanity from its modern and postmodern age.

There is a debate about the "boundaries of the Church" within each Christian denomination. As but one example, we find this tension in the Ukrainian Greek Catholic Church. On the one hand, in the 2016 document, *Ecumenical Concept of the Ukrainian Greek Catholic Church*, the ecumenical space-time is limited to baptized present-day Christians:

> Ecumenism (from the Greek οἰκουμένη, which means "the whole inhabited world") is the movement for the restoration of full unity among all Christians. Ecumenism, as such, only seeks the union of Christians, that is, of those who believe in the Holy Trinity, who are baptised in the name of the Father, the Son and the Holy Spirit, and who believe in the divine and human nature of our Lord, God and Saviour, Jesus Christ. The relations of Christians with followers of other religions or world views, in particular, new sects or religious movements, are not the subject of the present document.[7]

On the other hand, the same Ukrainian Greek-Catholic Church affirms, through the voice of its Major Archbishop,

---

[7] Ukrainian Greek-Catholic Church, *The Ecumenical Position of the Ukrainian Greek Catholic Church* (Lvov: Kolesso, 2016), no. 26.

in 2019, in his pastoral letter *Our Saint Sophia*, that the Church is a sophianic reality and therefore open to all. This interpretation holds that the Church is the actualization of the Wisdom of God, a biblical figure that represents God's life and appears in the book of Proverbs. Here the Church-Wisdom goes beyond the boundaries of confessional identities and, in every age, addresses all the sons of Adam:

> The Church of Sophia is a holy land of reconciliation and understanding, always open to universal unity of the children of God scattered throughout the world. For the Wisdom of God knows no bounds; she is always the same and embraces everyone and everything, "reaches mightily from one end of the earth to the other and she orders all things well" (Wisdom 8:1).[8]

This contradiction can only be resolved by taking into account the ecumenical nature of the Church. This point is crucial, because it allows the concerns of the world to be included, or not, within the reflection of theologians. In short, if the limits of the Church were to end with the sanctuary, the question of existing divisions within American or French society would not be the concern of metaphysics. To take just one example, if we consider it significant from an ecclesial viewpoint that the former American president, Joseph Biden, declared his Catholic beliefs in the face of his opponent, who claimed to be "non-denominational," we recognize that politics cannot ignore theology. Yet political science must find its ecumenical foundations.

The most important point to remember from the outset is the following: just as the Church is a reality that has

---

[8] "Our Saint Sophia Letter of His Beatitude Sviatoslav on the Occasion of the Centenary of the Renewal of Unity of the Ukrainian Nation and State." See https://ugcc.ua (last accessed August 5, 2025).

several meanings, as theologians Avery Dulles and Sergei
Bulgakov have shown, so the term *oikoumene* also has several different historical meanings that reflect distinct levels
of consciousness. This was authoritatively demonstrated in
1953 by the Dutch Reformed theologian Wilhem Visser't
Hooft (1900–1985), the first General Secretary of the
World Council of Churches, in his book, *The Meaning
of Ecumenical.*[9]

Firstly, for Herodotus, the word *oikoumene* meant the
whole world inhabited by men and, by extension, the
whole of humanity. One finds this same meaning of civilization in Demosthenes and Aristotle. From the conquests of Alexander the Great, in the fourth century BC,
the concept became more restricted, and designated the
Hellenized world, as opposed to the barbarian regions,
where the inhabitants could not be understood. The
term *oikoumene* took on a strong political connotation.
The *oikoumene* from that time on referred to the Roman
Empire, and later to the Byzantine Empire. Similarly,
whereas in the Septuagint the term *oikoumene* applied
to the whole of the cultivated land (as in Psalm 23), in
the Gospel, the term is employed when referring to the
Roman Empire, for example when Augustus orders a
census to be taken throughout the whole inhabited land
(*oikoumene*) (see Lk 2:1).

Thirdly, the term used by the author of the epistle to
the Hebrews takes on a radically new meaning when he
indicates that God has entrusted the *oikoumene to come*
to Christ and not to angels: "for it was not to angels
that God subjected the world to come [*oikoumene*] of
which we are speaking" (Heb 2:5). Here the *oikoumene*
to come means the Kingdom of God, announced by
"signs and wonders, miracles of all kinds" accomplished

---

[9] W. Visser't Hooft, *The Meaning of Ecumenical* (London: SCM
Press, 1953).

on earth by Jesus Christ, as opposed to the present *oik-oumene* which is perishable. Thus, the term has a double meaning: geographical universality, and the fullness of the Kingdom in spirit and in truth. For this reason, the term "oikoumene" is associated with both the Church and Catholicity in the minds of the Fathers of the Church, starting with Origen and Basil the Great. In Book XXII of the *City of God*, Augustine speaks of the *orbis terrarum* (the Latin term for *oikoumene*) of the Christian world as the true world.

Avery Dulles reminds us, in *The Catholicity of the Church*, that the term *Kath' hôlon* means "according to the whole." The Church is a configuration of the personal and relational whole of the Trinity. In the book of Acts, Luke refers to catholicity as both a geographical and spiritual category. "So the church throughout all Judea and Galilee and Samaria had peace and was built up; and walking in the fear of the Lord and in the comfort of the Holy Spirit it was multiplied" (Acts 9:31). In the second century, at the time of Ignatius of Antioch, in every local Church one finds the *catholica*. The bishop of Antioch writes in the Epistle to the Christians of Smyrna: "Wherever the bishop shall appear, there let the multitude [of the people] also be; even as, wherever Jesus Christ is, there is the Catholic Church" (Smyr., 8:2). Thus, the term *katholike* was understood in a fractal way. We know that a fractal is a mathematical shape that has a similar structure at all scales. The Church, understood as the apostolic community of local churches, was therefore different from the more political notion of the particular Church as part of a whole. At the beginning of the fifteenth century, the political consciousness of the Church had not erased the symbolic consciousness of Christians, even if the Byzantine interpretation of the *oikoumene* closely associated the Church with the political power of the Empire. Catholicity and ecumenicity were still considered compatible terms, despite the recurring tensions on this subject between patriarch and pope. Thus, the three confessions of faith of the early Church were called the *tria symbola catholica sive œcumenica* by the Reformation.

However, the divisions among Christians at the turn of the fifteenth and sixteenth centuries broke the existing identity between the terms "ecumenical" and "Catholic." The Roman Church designated itself as "Catholic" in the name of the "universal" mission granted by Christ to the apostle Peter, who became Bishop of Rome. The Eastern Church insisted on its "ecumenical" conception of the Church and the See of Constantinople, because of its fidelity to the first "Ecumenical Councils," and identified itself as "Orthodox." The churches of the "Reformation," meanwhile, hostile to a hermetic conception of Petrine apostolicity, posited fidelity to the Scriptures as the fundamental criterion of their identity.

It was not until the nineteenth century, and the founding of the Evangelical Alliance in London in 1846, that a fourth meaning of the term *oikoumene* emerged, one that was both interdenominational and international. The term had already been used in a new sense in the eighteenth century by the Lutheran theologian and Bishop of the Church of the Moravian Brethren, Nicolas-Louis Count of Zinzendorf (1700–1760), leader of the Unity of Brethren communities.

After the *oikoumene* as "inhabited land," as "political space of imperial domination," and the *oikoumene* as "chronotope of the revelation of the Kingdom of God on earth," the term has come to refer to "the movement of reconciliation among Christians," first within the Churches of the Reformation, most aware of the anti-evangelical nature of their divisions, and then, progressively, in the twentieth century, within the Christian world as a whole. By extension, from the end of the twentieth century onwards,

the term has been increasingly used to refer to the move‑
ment of interreligious and interconfessional reconciliation.
Indeed, the steady collapse of the modern conception of
the Church as subordinate to the sovereignty of the state,
according to the adage *cujus regio, ejus religio*, enabled the
Churches to reclaim their universal mission, both chari‑
table and missionary. Thus, for example, Henry Dunant,
founder of the International Red Cross, was also one of
the pioneers of the YMCA and secretary of the Evangel‑
ical Alliance in Geneva. As early as 1920, the Orthodox
and Anglican Churches joined initiatives for Christian
reconciliation and a new conception of international order.
Following the First World War, each Church was encour‑
aged, most notably in Stockholm in 1925 during the ecu‑
menical conference "Life and Work," by individuals like
Archbishop Nathan Söderblom of Uppsala, to consider
its own universality, sometimes in confrontation, some‑
times in dialogue, but always in "movement" with other
religious and denominational traditions. In 1937, when
the ecumenical movement was planning the creation of a
World Council of Churches, Father Yves Congar, a French
Dominican, published his book *Chrétiens désunis: prin‑
cipes d'un œcuménisme catholique* (*Divided Christendom:
a Catholic Study of the Problem of Reunion*).[10] He was a
driving force behind the Catholic Church's acceptance of
the ecumenical movement, as an inter‑confessional move‑
ment, during the Second Vatican Council (1962–1965).

For Visser't Hooft, there is a fifth, more metaphysical
meaning of the notion of *oikoumene*, made timely to a
large extent by the extraordinary proliferation of inter‑
religious and inter‑confessional encounters that have taken
place for more than half a century.[11] This last meaning

---

[10] *Divided Christendom: a Catholic Study of the Problem of Reunion*,
trans. M. A. Bousfield (London: Bles, 1939).
[11] *The Meaning of Ecumenical*: https://archive.org/details/mean‑
ingofecumeniooooviss (last accessed August 5, 2025).

expresses "the awareness and desire for Christian unity beyond any form of denominationalism." One finds this concern in many Churches today, in the Eastern Catholic Churches of the Middle East for example. Indeed, dialogues are meaningful only if they manage to arrive at original openings after extensive listening and sincere engagement. In this way, ecumenists have come to think of the relation between identity, difference, and communion in a ternary way. The meaning of *oikoumene* has become so spiritualized that Visser't Hooft came to speak of an "ecumenical faith." He explained this development through the tenacious memory in the Christian conscience of 1 Corinthians 12:13: "For by one Spirit we were all baptized into one body—Jews or Greeks, slaves or free—and all were made to drink of one Spirit." From this awareness of the *oikoumene* as the main characteristic of Christian faith-reason, the term *oikoumene* will be relative to the Spirit. It does not solely depend on the civilizational and political space, nor the temporal vision of the future Kingdom, nor the movement of rapprochement of ecclesial institutions. From now on, it points to a new metaphysics, open to all spiritual horizons and all forms of rational thought. One can link this awareness of the fifth meaning of *oikoumene* to Christ's words at the third epiphany of the voice of the Father in Jerusalem, described in John 12:28–29. Jesus Christ explains what has happened to his disciples in this way: "Now is the time for judgment on this world; now the prince of this world will be driven out. And I, when I am lifted up from the earth, will draw all people to myself" (Jn 12:31–32).

This contemporary conception of ecumenism extends the notion of *oikoumene* in space, in public life, in time, in relationships and in spiritual depths. It is rooted in the deepening of the personal dimension of the divine oneness in Western thought. It also owes much to the Eastern representations of Wisdom, in God, in nature and in man. It was, in addition, promoted by a certain number of thinkers conscious of the limits of scientistic and positivist rationality. All these contributions have allowed us to appreciate the truths, but also the limits, of nominalist thinking, which, by virtue of considering concepts as mere human constructs, have come to suppress the universal reality that they represent. The collective reflection also highlighted the element of truth in nihilist thought, its rejection of the position seeking refuge behind the scene of ideas. However, it also underlined its falsehood, the assertion whereby "there is no truth since being does not exist." In fact, this new definition of ecumenism proposes a renewed framework of the relations between belief and knowledge, between God and man, between Wisdom and being, between the person and the individual. Ecumenical is that which seeks and brings to light a "unified and pluralistic" relationship to the world, capable of thinking peacefully together the beautiful and the true, the good and the just.

It is therefore easier to understand the different interpretations of ecumenism that exist between the Churches, within the Churches, and outside the Churches. Some may regard ecumenism as an intra-religious ideology with little to do with science or the real world, since no concept can grasp absolute realities, and revealed truths cannot generate "living together." Others may declare themselves to be ecumenical while consciously or unconsciously understanding universality in a primarily political, social or environmental way. There are, of course, those who reject ecumenism because of their relativistic and consensualist perception of the movement. These factors, in their view, prevent any affirmation of the full and whole truth they advocate. Others, finally, pronounce themselves, more subtly, both for and against ecumenism. They recognize the mission of Churches to bear witness to love between them, according to the model of reconciled diversity, in the image of the life of the Trinity. However, when it comes to making a personal decision that could limit the freedom of their confession, they begin to equivocate, which contributes to weakening the dynamics of the ecumenical movement. These positions clash because of the absence of a fully-fledged science of ecumenism. This science is only founded on a higher level of consciousness, that of ecumenical metaphysics.

2

A Short History of Ecumenical Metaphysics

ETAPHYSICS has a very long history. Aristotle had already concluded in the fourth century BC that it was appropriate to make room for a science capable of understanding the being "in its entirety," following the study of physical reality. Therefore, the primary trait of metaphysics has always been that it considers itself to be *katholou*, or universal. Later, in the Middle Ages, metaphysics was defined as the science that articulated in a single discourse the representations that humans make of nature, its origin, and destiny, as well as of themselves. The metaphysics of today is redefined as a deeply religious view of the world, as demonstrated by Pope John Paul II in *Fides et ratio* (1998) and the academic Catherine Pickstock, a professor at the University of Cambridge, in *Aspects of Truth* (2020). For it alone is ready to defend the possibility of a true discourse, capable of uniting in glory the good and the just, by virtue of its ability to open itself through faith to what transcends the space-time of being.[1]

CRITIQUE OF MODERN PHILOSOPHY AND THEOLOGY

The error of mediaeval metaphysics, mostly resulting from the influence of Scottish theologian and philosopher John Duns Scotus (1266–1308), consisted, in a nutshell, in uniformly identifying the divine with the natural. Metaphysics loses its dogmatic nature, in the etymological sense of the term, that is, its ability to provide symbolic boundaries to the experience of truth within which a living

---

[1] C. Pickstock, *Aspects of Truth: A New Religious Metaphysics* (Cambridge: Cambridge University Press, 2020).

encounter between man and being might occur, until it reaches divine and absolute reality. The term "dogmatism" took on a new meaning when it came to the method of applying the Absolute to concepts. This monistic approach helped to explain the divine being's supreme power. The vision gave rise to the deist reaction of the Enlightenment. In order to release God from the injustices of history, He is disassociated from the affairs of this world.

The other effect of this representation was to portray the divine unity in an abstract and material form. In particular, after Saint Thomas Aquinas, academic thinkers conceptualized being as a stable and available presence rather than a dynamic and responsive one, as it was for the first-millennium Fathers of the Church. For modern thinkers such as Spinoza, Leibniz, and Descartes, prior mathematical reasonings might be applied to the world of the Spirit. Knowing oneself, according to them, entailed having complete certainty, comparable to that found in the experience of faith. The foundation of modern knowledge should be built on close examination of verifiable evidence that is shared by all people, regardless of their level of consciousness. However, this certainty was only based on the subject's thinking. It was deprived of any dynamic that might have connected people to a spiritual community and to the transcendent Being.

Descartes' representation of the self as a substance that can exist on its own led to the dualism of the mind and body. The body, which was made of material matter, was called upon to die and decompose, whereas the soul, which is the substance of thought, is entirely spiritual and hence cannot be extended. This metaphysics, which contradicts the grand patristic image of the human person as a microcosm of body, soul, and spirit, leads to non-orthodox representations of God. Baruch Spinoza attempts to transcend the Cartesian dualism of extension and thought by developing the concept of "unique substance." However, as noted by the philosopher Lev Shestov, for Spinoza, this unique substance would no longer have anything personal about it and ordered everything with the same necessity. Consequently, a Creator God of heaven and earth who had willingly created free man could not possibly exist.

It is known that the philosopher Immanuel Kant (1724–1804) attempted to liberate metaphysics from this atheistic idea through a renewed metaphysics. He fundamentally distinguished the domain of phenomena from that of noumena in order to liberate the person from any power that the world of objects held over them. At the end of his life, in 1798, in *The Conflict of the Faculties*, Kant even challenged the division established within the university between the sphere of rationality (considered inferior and belonging to philosophy) and the sphere of faith (considered superior and pertinent to theology). As the philosopher of pure reason, he explained that he was also a Lutheran believer who longed to debate with theologians of other Christian confessions ... The mistake was that, at the time, theological rationality was entirely dependent on political power, which prevented modern thought from opening up to religious philosophy.

However, the Lutheran thinker eventually came to deny the role of intuition in metaphysical knowledge, owing to the fact that the real world (of things in themselves) had become unknowable in contrast to the nonreal world of phenomena. Conversely, according to the Russian philosopher Nicolas Berdyaev (1874–1958), there is neither pure thought nor pure reason, because thought is infused with emotions and desires. They play a decisive role in knowledge, sometimes negatively, but also positively.

> It was a fundamental mistake in Kant that he recognized sensuous experience, in which appearances are the data, but he did not recognize spiritual experience, of which the data are noumenal. Man remains, as it were, corked up in the world

of phenomena; he is unable to break out of it, or
able to break out only by way of practical postulates. Kant regarded man as, from man's point
of view, an appearance; man was not revealed to
himself as a noumenon.[2]

This is why the Kantian breach was interpreted by its
interpreters as a split between faith and reason. Georg
Wilhelm Friedrich Hegel (1770–1831) ignited the rebellion.
His *Phenomenology of Spirit* (1807) aimed to help Lutheran
theology redefine the science of being from the ground
up. In order to transcend Kantian duality, reason becomes
divine. However, his monist view of the Spirit leads to
an absolute ontology, an identification of theology with
ontology. However, according to Berdyaev, there was no
such thing as an objective spirit, merely the objectivation
or a distortion of spirit. Spirit, which is freedom, reveals
itself throughout history, but only eschatologically, and
through every act of creative inspiration. According to
Berdyaev, God is Spirit, and cannot be objectified by some
formula that would necessarily reduce his nature to what
can be perceived by human concepts:

> But the Hegelian universal monism failed for
> this reason, that the Absolute is actualized in the
> form of absolute necessity. Because of that, how-
> ever much Hegel may have talked about freedom,
> he does not know freedom. Hegel asserts the
> identity of spirit with philosophy, his own, the
> Hegelian philosophy. This is the most dreadful
> philosophical pride which the history of phi-
> losophy knows [...]. What was fundamentally
> wrong about those idealist systems of metaphys-
> ics was their monism, which is an impossible
> thing within the limits of a fallen world, their
> mistaken, anti-personalist conception of freedom.[3]

---

[2] N. Berdiaeff, *Essai de métaphysique eschatologique* (Paris: Aubier,
1947), 22.
[3] Ibid., 35.

The German philosopher Martin Heidegger (1889–1966) rejected both the sharing of Kantian spheres and the positioning of the self within Hegelian theological discourse. For him, the authoritative and unjust metaphysics of modernity had stifled the genuine experience of being. The Kantian theory of knowledge, meanwhile, could only lead to positivism, since it treated all reality as a scientific object. This is why contemporary metaphysics could only be understood at the time through the personification of a brand-new deity called the *Technik* [technology], whose goal was complete control over minds. Heidegger also believed that modern metaphysics needed to be dismantled or, as Jacques Derrida would later say, deconstructed.

This deconstruction of current metaphysics was particularly critical of post-Thomistic thought. The loss of the *actus essendi*, still present with Thomas Aquinas, has led Western Christian theology, particularly that of Suarez and Cajetan, to lose the biblical and patristic sense of created Wisdom, to reduce it to a simple vertu, to forget its foundation in divine Wisdom, and, as a result, fundamentally to separate human nature from the divine supernatural. The main currents of contemporary thought, such as conceptualism, rationalism, and idealism, are the result of this forgetting of the sapiential dimension of being. So, it was either limited to singularity, as in nominalism, or it was nothing more than whatever the mind chose to imagine, as in voluntarism. This rationalist trend in modern philosophy emphasized the contradiction between faith and reason, and precipitated the division of Christians into three major confessions: Catholic, Protestant, and Orthodox. In the absence of a religious philosophy capable of thinking together the various polarities of metaphysical rationality, as well as the various aspects of orthodox Christian faith, truth has been reduced to what can be grasped from immutable and certain human *cogito* (for philosophical interpretation) and the paradigm of faithful memory (for theological interpretation). Modern theologians identified the criteria for truth as being found in either the Magisterium (for Catholics), the Scriptures (for Protestants), or the Tradition of the Ecumenical Councils, (for the Orthodox).[4] It took decades of ecumenical dialogues for the major contemporary theologians of various confessions to recognize that the "supreme rule" of their faith, according to the first statement of conscience of the "anti-modern" First Vatican Council, "comes from the unity that the Spirit has made between the Holy Tradition, Holy Scripture, and the Holy Magisterium of the Church, in such a way that the three cannot exist independently."[5]

CRITIQUE OF POSTMODERN THOUGHT

With his attributes of truth, totality, and homogeneity, Friedrich Nietzsche (1844–1900) was the first to denounce the pretended absoluteness of modern metaphysics. He also claimed an extravagant amount of power to judge, measure, and even save people from an unstable and deceitful world. The German philosopher established a line of continuity between the Aristotelian substance and the Cartesian theory of the self-sufficient subject: in both cases, being required only itself to exist. The ecstatic temporality of self-consciousness was disregarded.

Following Nietzsche, postmodern thought had the merit of undermining this self-assurance of conceptual rationality. As stated by philosopher Francis Guibal:

> for a thought that is willing to put its finality to
> the test, or to know and desire the expression

---

[4] A. Arjakovsky, *What is Orthodoxy?* (New York: Angelico Press, 2018).

[5] "... by divine and Catholic faith, all those things must be believed which are contained in the written word of God and in tradition, and those which are proposed by the Church, either in a solemn pronouncement or in her ordinary and universal teaching power, to be believed as divinely revealed." *Dei Filius*, April 24, 1870.

of a subject originally dedicated to the sharing of the world and its history, being and meaning manifest themselves not through an objective abstraction (classical metaphysics), nor through a subjective construction (modern metaphysics), but only through a renewed vision that is willing to welcome and follow the various forms of experience in their ineffable contingency and immanent meaning.[6]

The historical purpose of the idea of the distinction between a being and Being was to first demonstrate the inconsistencies and deficiencies of the Hegelian theory of the one totality. The emphasis on what resists the allure of the Great All in the name of existential imperatives was accompanied by a reminder of the personal character of Being. Indeed, for the Romanian philosopher Benjamin Fondane (1898–1944), curing a paralytic or feeding the hungry takes precedence over historical and philosophical concerns.

Postmodern thought also challenged the supposedly immutable, clear and distinct, obligatory and binding nature of modern truths. Thus, for the French philosopher Jacques Derrida (1930–2004), the mysterious was not necessarily incompatible with truth. On the other hand, the Austrian philosopher Karl Popper (1902–1994) demonstrated that scientific practice excluded the scientistic dream of absolute objectivity. Chestov, for his part, reminds us that truth is not necessarily subject to necessity, as revealed by the "metaphysics of the Exodus" highlighted by Étienne Gilson. According to this view, truth depends above all on the will of God. Ontotheological thought had consisted, from the fourteenth century onwards, in reducing God to his concept, under the successive and compatible titles of *causa sui, ens summe perfectum* and

---

[6] F. Guibal, *Faut-il renoncer à la métaphysique?* (Paris: Éd. des facultés jésuites, 2016), 114.

"moral god." For the French philosopher Jean-Luc Marion, this elaboration, precisely because it brought God to the univocal rationality of the concept, resulted in an idol, identified as such by Nietzsche.[7]

Postmodern philosophers, from Jean-Paul Sartre to Michel Foucault, reject the theodicy of German mathematician and philosopher Gottfried Leibniz (1646–1716), as well as that of French philosopher and theologian Nicolas Malebranche (1638–1715), that is, modern philosophical forms of God's justification with respect to the question of innocent suffering.

Russian religious thought's critique of Western philosophy, but also Martin Heidegger's criticism of the phenomenology of his master Edmond Husserl, restored in the twentieth century a more complex vision of the mystery of divine-humanity, an eschatological consideration of being and a Trinitarian sophiology.

The doctrine of salvation was considerably renewed by Russian religious philosophy. It had the great merit of finding a response at once rational and spiritual to the impasses of modern and postmodern thought. Nicholas Berdyaev questioned neither the reality of evil nor the omnipotence of God. He simply placed the latter at a different level from that of the objectified world. As a personalist thinker, Berdyaev was sensitive to the interactions between the Divine Spirit and the human spirit. This is what the Russian philosopher wrote on this subject in his *Essay on Eschatological Metaphysics*:

> To bring belief in God within the bounds of possibility and to make it morally possible to accept him, can only be done by recognizing the truth that God reveals himself in this world. He reveals himself in the prophets, in his Son, in the breath of the Spirit and in the uplifting spiritual

---

[7] J.-L. Marion, "Les limites de la phénoménalité," in *Ce peu d'espace autour* (Paris: Éd. de la Transparence, 2010), 21.

aspirations of men. But God does not govern this world, the world of objectivity which is under the power of its own Prince — the "Prince of this world." God is not "the world," and the revelation of God in the world is an eschatological revelation. God is not in the world, that is, not in its given factuality and its necessity, but in its setting of a task and in its freedom. *God is present*, and God acts, only in freedom. *He is not present*, nor does he act, in necessity. God is to be found in Truth, in Goodness, Beauty and Love, but not in the world order. God shows himself in the world in truth and right, but he does not dominate over it in virtue of his power. God is Spirit and he can operate only in Spirit and through Spirit. Our ideas about power, about authority and causality are entirely inapplicable to God. The mystery of God's operation in the world and in man usually finds expression in the doctrine of grace, and grace bears no resemblance to what we understand by necessity, power, authority and causality; our conception of these is derived from the world. For this reason alone grace cannot be set in antithesis to freedom — it is combined with freedom.[8]

This emerging theodicy allows a new generation of philosophers to respond to criticisms of Nietzsche's and Heidegger's Judeo-Christian thought and to demonstrate the limitations of their philosophical systems. Emmanuel Lévinas (1906–1995) reintroduced Nicolas Berdyaev's main thesis in his famous book *Totalité et infinité* (1961). The subjectivism of the French philosopher of Lithuanian descent stood in opposition to Husserl's objectivism, which was based on intentionality as appropriateness to the object of thought. It was a personal subjectivism in

---

[8] Berdiaeff, *Essai de métaphysique eschatologique* (Paris: Aubier, 1946), 174–75. N. Berdyaev, *Essay on Eschatological Metaphysics, The Beginning and the End* (New York: Harper Torchbook, 1957), part 3, chap. 5, para. 151.

the sense that it derived its basis from the concept of
infinity in an asymmetric way:

> Eschatology institutes a relation with being
> *beyond the totality* or beyond history, and not
> with being beyond the past and present. Not
> with the void that would surround the totality
> and where one could, arbitrarily, think what one
> likes, and thus promote the claims of a subjec-
> tivity free as the wind. It is a relationship with
> *a surplus always exterior to the totality*, as though
> the objective totality did not fill out the true
> measure of being, as though another concept,
> the concept of *infinity*, were needed to express
> this transcendence with regard to totality, non-
> encompassable within a totality and as primordial
> as totality. This "beyond" the totality and objec-
> tive experience is, however, not to be described
> in a purely negative fashion. It is reflected *within*
> the totality and history, *within* experience. The
> eschatological, as the "beyond" of history, draws
> beings out of the jurisdiction of history and the
> future; it arouses them in and calls them forth
> to their full responsibility.[9]

Emmanuel Levinas, as well as Lev Shestov and Nicolas
Berdyaev before him, reproached Husserl's phenomenology
for having only an abstract representation of consciousness.
Yet the vision of essences through the discovery of pure
consciousness does not reveal the mystery of existence.
Authentic metaphysics, on the other hand, is personalist,
eschatological, and admits the sophianic source of being.
Since it recognizes the existence of the subject, and its
capacity to participate in spiritual being, human knowledge is capable of illuminating being from its own light.
Contemporary phenomenology, even when most open to
spirituality, has difficulty admitting that human rationality

---

[9]   E. Lévinas, *Totalité et infini, Essai sur l'extériorité* (Leyde: M.
Nijhof, 1961), 6; E. Levinas, *Totality and Infinity, An Essay on
Exteriority* (Duquesne University Press, 1969), 22–23.

can participate in divine rationality. It is therefore led to disguise a metaphysics that is frequently symbolic and intuitive, as in the case of Jean-Luc Marion, by the expression "phenomenology of revelation."[10] Despite the fact that this methodological agnosticism is contradictory and, in particular, prevents one from stating the personal source of the contribution, it nevertheless makes it possible to reintroduce a properly sophiological discourse into philosophy:

> How might the mystery of God's kingdom allow phenomenalization? The first occasion recorded by 1 Corinthians identifies the impetus from which the phenomenon known as the *mustêrion* of wisdom arose, "wisdom, a *mustêrion* that has been hidden" (1 Cor 2:7) so that it is initially defined negatively with contrast to "the wisdom of this age" (2:6) that which is put into practise by the masters of this world. Indeed, the wisdom of God remains hidden until it is discovered in oneself by the very Spirit of God [...]. God revealed it [Wisdom] to us (*apekalupsen*) by his Spirit, because "the Spirit searches everything, even the depths of God" (2: 9–10 citing Is 64:3). To discover the mystery of the kingdom, we must transfer our spirit to the Spirit of God, moving from one to the other, in order to see the *mustêrion* as God reveals it: It is nothing more than a reversal of intentionality: casting God's intentional gaze upon God rather than remaining focused upon our intentionality when the intuition of the *mustêrion* arises.[11]

On the theologians' side, the Jesuit Henri de Lubac brought the anthropology of the Church Fathers back to light by restoring the uncreated desire of the created creature towards its creator. The French theologian resurrects the most fundamental concept of Christian metaphysics:

---

[10] J.-L. Marion, *D'ailleurs, la révélation* (Paris: Grasset, 2020), 185.
[11] Ibid., 307.

man's ability to participate in the creation of the world, the categorization of phenomena, and the coming of God's Kingdom on Earth. Sergei Bulgakov, on the other hand, has gone even further by proposing a sophiology that is both traditional and creative due to its firmly trinitarian nature. According to Bulgakov, the Thomist notion of ideas created by God and acting in the world had more in common with Plato and Aristotle than with the Christian doctrine of the Trinitarian act of creation. For Thomas Aquinas, God is a pure act, like Aristotle's Prime Mover, transcendent in relation to being.[12] However, this transcendence occurs according to the degree of perfection, not the divine essence. Aquinas himself admitted to understanding creation as a causal emanation. Yet, as the Russian theologian reminded us, to create is not to set in motion, as in the world's mechanical causality. Creating is a deeply personal act. According to Bulgakov, divine creation is an act of self-revelation by God in his created and uncreated Wisdom.

> The creation of the world is, first of all, a self-positing of God which exists in God together with His sophianic self-revelation. In essence, the creation cannot, of course, differ from this sophianic self-revelation. The creation of the world is included in God's sophianic self-positing and consists in the fact that the Divine being in Sophia receives *another being in the world*. The Divine Sophia exists in dual mode: in her own mode, which belongs to her in eternity; and in the creaturely mode, as the world.[13]

---

[12] Keith Lemna's remarkable work, *The Trinitarian Wisdom of God, Louis Bouyer's Theology of the God-World Relationship* (Emmaus Academic, 2023) shows, however, based on Stratford Caldecott's interpretation, that according to Saint Thomas Aquinas, the first gift of creation, created wisdom, is associated with the *esse commune* or *esse creatum*, the being common and present to all creations.

[13] S. Boulgakov, *L'Épouse de l'Agneau*, trans. Constantin Andronikof (Paris: L'Âge d'Homme, 1984), 42–43; S. Bulgakov, *The Bride of*

This sophiological metaphysics formulates an original concept of unity and diversity:

> The Divine Sophia is God's exhaustive self-revelation, the fullness of divinity, and therefore has absolute content. There can be no positive principle of being that does not enter into this fullness of sophianic life and revelation. The divine All belongs to the Divine Sophia; she is the all-unity of the divine All. [...] Every idea, element, or atom of being contemplated by the thought of the divine Word and illuminated by the life-giving power of the Holy Spirit is contained in the Divine Sophia. And to this multiplicity of fullness belongs the connection of multi-unity, all-unity. The unity does not revoke, swallow up, or weaken the multiplicity; nor does the multiplicity annul the unity. Sophia is integral wisdom and all-wisdom, all in all, and unity in multiplicity.[14]

THE NEW HORIZONS OF METAPHYSICS

Because of the rediscovery of personalism, sophiology, eschatology, and the ternary character of consciousness, contemporary metaphysics has increasingly assumed its ecumenical character, understood here as that which comes after the modern and confessional, postmodern and individualistic ages. This ecumenical dimension, understood also as a new relationship between truth and method, universality and personhood, has been particularly worked on by a number of thinkers, among them the German philosopher Hans-Georg Gadamer, the Irish philosopher William Desmond, and the French philosopher Francis Jacques.

Hans-Georg Gadamer (1900–2002) was Heidegger's assistant in Marburg in 1923–24. He played a decisive

---

the Lamb, trans. Boris Jakim (Grand Rapids, MI and Edinburgh: Wm. B. Eerdmans Publishing, 2001), 46.
[14] Ibid., 37, 39.

role in enabling contemporary philosophy to break away from modern scientism without abandoning its claim to speak the truth. The German philosopher identified himself as a Protestant Christian thinker. Furthermore, Gadamer did not hesitate to refer to Christian wisdom in an attempt to refound metaphysics on the basis of a dialogical hermeneutic. For him, hermeneutics refers to both the self-interpretation of existence and the reflection on this capacity for interpretation, that dialogue is meant to awaken. Based on Hölderlin's discovery that "we are a discourse," this discipline is for him profoundly ecumenical. In 1990, Hans-Georg Gadamer, then at the pinnacle of his national and international reputation, made a significant statement for ecumenical metaphysics: "We must learn to think in an ecumenical manner."[15]

In fact, according to Gadamer, the primitive Christian consciousness gave rise to this new type of hermeneutical knowledge, this ear, or "this sensibility to the imprints that reside in our concepts." According to this new representation of the process of understanding, the emergence of truth is found in the ability to hold together the heart and intelligence, as well as internal freedom and relational communal spirit. The ability to comprehend in this context differs from the desire to control, which is inherent in both traditional and modern modes of object knowledge. Whether it be the sciences of the mind or the natural sciences, it cannot be dissociated from "belief" as scientific thinkers would have it. The interpretive mind, and more precisely the questioning mind, becomes the vital characteristic of the mode of being of human beings in the world.

This discovery in the first instance concerned the Christian consciousness. The apostle Paul asked the Philippians

---

[15] H.-G. Gadamer, *La Philosophie herméneutique*, translation and notes by Jean Grondin (Paris: PUF, 1996), 226.

to fight the same battle of humility and obedience in the service of harmony that Christ had led "in the name of the Father." St Paul, in fact, affirms that God the Father has exalted Jesus Christ by giving him "the Name that is above every name" (Phil 2:9). In this exhortation we find a philosophy of the Name that Hans-Georg Gadamer sought to formalize in his book *Truth and Method*. The main characteristic of his philosophical hermeneutics is to consider language as the universal medium in which understanding itself takes place, which is realized in interpretation. Yet, if understanding is to interpret, it is because of the dialogical character of being and of the language that aims to express it. Interpretation is also, like conversation, a circle that presupposes a dialectic of questions and answers.

The rediscovery of the Platonic *metaxu*, of the in-between, of being as pure mediation, of the nuptial encounter between Created wisdom and Wisdom uncreated constitutes, for the Irish philosopher William Desmond, the key to a rediscovery of what he calls "the intimate strangeness of Being."[16] Instead of reducing the Absolute to the finite circularity of Logic, as with Hegel, it is appropriate to explore, according to him, a zone of ontological experience, situated between pure transcendence and the most empirical reality, where man experiences the event of "surplus immediacy" which the dialectical concept cannot explain. The rejection of univocity, equivocation, and false dialectic led to the experience of immanent transcendence, familiar alterity, and welcoming strangeness. For Desmond, then, we have to be, or exist, authentically in our relationship to what we are, as we are, dependent on being that gives itself to us at the same time it gives us to ourselves, while leaving

---

[16] W. Desmond, *The Intimate Strangeness of Being: Metaphysics After Dialectics* (Washington, DC: CUA Press, 2012).

us free to determine ourselves in action. This new ecumenical metaphysics of the in-between, as taught by
Desmond, or of love, as taught by Emmanuel Tourpe,
allows us to think creatively about the relationship
between unity and alterity, universality and singularity.
It separates itself from both the Manichaean dualism
and the Hegelian monism:

> There is a difference of a true monotheism, and
> any monism. Paradoxically, real monotheism, in
> affirming the singularity of God, is an affirma-
> tion of difference, not its reduction to unity. And
> the difference is not a fall from the One but
> a creation of divine generosity invested with
> its own power to be. The endowed creation is
> originated with the promise of its own original
> self-being, God does not have to become in order
> to be Godself. The logic of self-becoming is not
> appropriate to God, though this is not to deny
> a dynamic activity to God. This *actus essendi* is
> beyond coming to be, endowing finite coming
> to be and becoming.[17]

This renewal of metaphysical thought, therefore, has
important consequences for interreligious dialogue. Chinese wisdom, polarity thinking, does not separate the noun
from the adjective. It understands the world in antinomic
pairs (the word for landscape, for example, is "mountain-
water" in Chinese).[18] As soon as one frees oneself from
the framework of ontotheology, of the conceptual idolatry
of a God coinciding with himself in the clarity and distinction of the concept, one opens oneself simultaneously
to the interest of a thought of the in-betweenness, of
transition, of process, of life.

Francis Jacques, a philosopher and a member of the
Academy of Education and Social Studies, has proposed

---

[17] Ibid., 250.
[18] P. David, "Pour ouvrir des possibles," *En lisant François Jullien*,
ed. P. David and A. Riou (Paris: Lethielleux, 2012), 19.

an original understanding of truth based on the "erotetic" or interrogative method. This consists in constantly questioning, like children, to get closer to the truth.[19] Truth is understood in a broader and more complex manner than its mere scientific reduction. It is also grasped in a more vivid way than by postmodern thinkers. According to F. Jacques, "interrogative thought replaces inquiry at the service of doubt, introduced by René Descartes in the modern era, by inquiry at the service of truth."[20] The challenge is hence the truth of the doubt and its authenticity. This, in turn, restores faith. For believing does not erase the possibility of doubt, but rather displaces it. Faith begins with the awareness of one's lack of faith.[21]

This realization enables the recent history of the philosophy of truth to be explained. According to F. Jacques, this process involves three significant steps. After Duns Scotus's revolution, the traditional era believed that truth was one and indivisible, total, or non-existent. The revelation's truth was understood as a scientific fact. The modern era, on the other hand, has fragmented the truth following Kant. One could imagine several spheres of human existence and hence disciplines, each with its own method and goal. The postmodern era offers a mystical view of truth that rejects all forms of objectivity in favour of allowing everyone the freedom to create their own bricolages, if not manipulations. F. Jacques's thought can be extended by

---

[19] F. Jacques, "Une et plurielle: Pour une érotétique de la verité," *La vérité une et plurielle, Actes des journées de l'Association des philosophes chrétiens*, ed. F. Jacques (Paris: Lethielleux, 2010), 143–92.

[20] Ibid., 150.

[21] In the Gospel, a father sees his son, possessed by a mute spirit, healed by Christ. After seeing the spirit violently seize the child, Jesus asked his father "How long has he had this?" And he said, "From childhood. And it has often cast him into the fire and into the water, to destroy him; but if you can do anything, have pity on us and help us." And Jesus said to him, "If you can! All things are possible to him who believes." Immediately the father of the child cried out and said, "I believe; help my unbelief!" (Mk 9:14–29).

imagining a fourth level of consciousness, that of spiritual conscience. This level does not seek to possess the truth, nor to dilute it, but to listen to it and to approach it by way of eminence, by concentric circles, by levels of consciousness, in order to draw meaning, coherence, harmony and joy. It brings the human spirit into contact with the epiphanies of the divine.

The truth is therefore ecumenical, both one and many. There are various approaches to truth, and several ways to access its symphonic dimension via the interrogative path. With Francis Jacques, the following schema of its unfolding can be summarized. From Aristotle to Hegel, truth has been understood fundamentally as correspondence, conformity of representation to the object, of the rational and the real. But Wittgenstein showed the limit of this approach since "the correspondence between an assertion and a fact must itself be the subject of an assertion, whose correspondence with the corresponding fact must itself be the subject of another assertion and so on ad infinitum." [22] For St Augustine, truth is an enduring reality, *the unity* of all that is true, as well as *one's own identity as something that proves stable and permanent* over the course of time. From the logical positivist Rudolf Carnap (1891–1970) to the former president of the American Catholic Philosophy Association, Nicholas Rescher (born 1928), truth has been understood first *as coherence, as the ability to reconcile different theories or even different objects.* The truth of a particular statement is where it sits in the overall discourse or if it allows for the reception of meaning by enshrining itself in a horizon of totalization. This approach is similar to the truth-consensus approach, in that coherence is the foundation of agreement among those who judge. The main distinction is that, according to pragmatism, truth does not exist in itself. It is gradually revealed through

---

[22] Ibid., 154.

experience. For its promoter, the American semiologist and philosopher Charles Sanders Peirce (1839–1914), "a proposition presumed to be true is one that has been the subject of a consensus tested by confrontation and open to refutation."

Thus, from a philosophical aspect, we find the main characteristics of the four major paradigms of orthodoxy of the Christian faith (worthy glorification, right truth, faithful memory, true and just knowledge) as revealed by historical analysis.[23] Indeed, glorification is inextricably linked to intellect, which seeks to align judgment and reality, and hence interiorization and expressiveness. Right truth is based on the concern for coherence between a particular proposition and the meaning it acquires in a total discourse, but also between what is said and what is done. Truth as true and just knowledge is turned towards the quest for conciliar consensus, while faithful memory is concerned with the stability and unity of truth.

In response to this multipolar conception of truth, modern rationality, notably from Francis Bacon onwards, has partially (that is, in the original sense of the word, "heretically") introduced the understanding of truth as success and effectiveness, and the interpretation of faith as a mere personal belief disconnected from reality. In this logic, whatever seeks to prove itself by making itself true becomes superior to what simply is. The limit here is to believe that modeling a reality will exhaust it. This rationality privileges the superficiality of being. By cutting itself off from any relation to wisdom, it comes to disconnect itself from any sense of virtue and from any dynamic participation in the life of the Logos. It also distances itself from Gospel revelation. In fact, Christ reveals to his disciples the personal, relational, and participatory

---

[23] See A. Arjakovsky, *What is Orthodoxy?* (Brooklyn, NY: Angelico Press, 2018).

dimension of truth: "I am the way, and the truth, and the life" (Jn 14:6).

On the basis of this awareness, contemporary ecumenical metaphysics seeks to understand how the integrity of faith is degraded by dissociating knowledge and truth, memory and glory, but also consensus and coherence, stability and correspondence. The uniqueness of ecumenical metaphysics is therefore to understand the true participation of living beings in terms of the levels of consciousness to which they have access. This is why it is now necessary to present the main principles of this new metaphysics.

3

Principles of an Ecumenical Science

CUMENICAL metaphysics is based on a new conception of the universal, in the first instance through its questioning of the ancient rules of logic. Let us begin with an overview of how contemporary metaphysics has freed itself from binary logic. Philosophical thought, since Aristotle, has been based on the principles of identity, non-contradiction and excluded third. This means that all reality is equal to itself, that one cannot say one thing and its opposite and there is no third term that is both A and not A. Rational binary thought, based on these principles, relies on the adequation of the thing to the intellect, and on "proof," understood as the explanation of a phenomenon by its universalizable repetition. According to the philosopher Lev Shestov, this worldview is a form of naivety in relation to the non-dual organization of reality. In the binary view, man, who nevertheless has infinite dignity, must submit to the order and appearance that phenomena are willing to give of themselves. This is a form of passivity that leads to fatalism or war. This form of phenomenological thinking leads to *a priori* judgments that force us to understand all reality as something abstract and uniform. It therefore forbids the consideration of truth as the fruit of personal experience.

Conversely, as demonstrated by the American philosopher David Bentley Hart, ternary metaphysics allows us to describe the realization of the unity and wholeness of all existence.[1] Since it knows how to distinguish in

---

[1] D. B. Hart, *The Experience of God: Being, Consciousness, Bliss* (New Haven and London: Yale University Press, 2013).

an antinomic way God, understood as Spirit, uncreated
and totally free with regard to our representations of
space and time, from the naturalistic representation of
God, understood only as a cosmic power, it offers a platform for encounter between the main theistic traditions
of the world, but also with certain aspects of Buddhism
and Taoism. This ternary approach, which should not be
confused with the properly Trinitarian vision of Christian
theology, allows us to think of Being, Consciousness and
Fulfillment together, whether based on the philosophy
of Vedanta or on those of Jewish mysticism (the latter
speaks of the Hokhma, as an uncreated reality, both "in
God" and "outside of God" and the Shekinah which sig-
nifies the presence of God in the world), Muslim mysticism (Ibn Arabi used the formula *wujud* [Being], *wijdan*
[consciousness], and *wajd* [fulfillment] to present God as
absolute Reality) or Christian mysticism (Henri le Saux,
the Benedictine monk who adopted the name of Swami
Abhishiktananda, used the formula "Sat, Chit, Ananda" to
describe his personal experience of God). David Bentley
Hart emphasized the fundamental distinction between the
world's major categories of religious metaphysics, united by
this ternary approach, and the materialist or naturalistic
philosophies, which conceive of God as a demiurge and
ultimately proclaim his non-existence:

> To speak of "God" properly, then — to use the
> word in a sense consonant with the teachings
> of orthodox Judaism, Christianity, Islam, Sikh-
> ism, Hinduism, Bahá'í, a great deal of antique
> paganism, and so forth — is to speak of the one
> infinite source of all that is: eternal, omniscient,
> omnipotent, omnipresent, uncreated, uncaused,
> perfectly transcendent of all things and for that
> very reason absolutely immanent to all things.
> God so understood is not something posed over
> against the universe, in addition to it, nor is he
> the universe itself. He is not a "being," at least not

in the way that a tree, a shoemaker, or a god is a being; he is not one more object in the inventory of things that are, or any sort of discrete object at all. Rather, all things that exist receive their being continuously from him, who is the infinite wellspring of all that is, in whom (to use the language of the Christian scriptures) all things live and move and have their being. In one sense he is "beyond being," if by being one means the totality of discrete, finite things. In another sense he is "being itself," in that he is the inexhaustible source of all reality, the absolute upon which the contingent is always utterly dependent, the unity and simplicity that underlies and sustains the diversity of finite and composite things. Infinite being, infinite consciousness, infinite bliss, from whom we are, by whom we know and are known, and in whom we find our only true consummation. All the great theistic traditions agree that God, understood in this proper sense, is essentially beyond finite comprehension; hence, much of the language used of him is negative in form and has been reached only by a logical process of abstraction from those qualities of finite reality that make it insufficient to account for its own existence. All agree as well, however, that he can genuinely be known: that is, reasoned toward, intimately encountered, directly experienced with a fulness surpassing mere conceptual comprehension.[2]

God is the only act of being, of self-consciousness, and of fulfillment, in whom everything lives, moves and receives its being. This is why, even if the terms must always be differentiated and contextualized according to cultures and times, the only way to know the truth of things in the great metaphysical traditions[3] is the path of fulfillment.

The soul's unquenchable eros for the divine, of which Plotinus and Gregory of Nyssa and

---

[2] Ibid., 30–31.
[3] Ibid., 248.

countless Christian contemplatives speak, Sufism's
'ishq or passionately adherent love for God, Jewish mysticism's devekut, Hinduism's bhakti, Sikh-
ism's pyaar—these are all names for the acute
manifestation of a love that, in a more chronic
and subtle form, underlies all knowledge, all
openness of the mind to the truth of things.

At this level of consciousness, knowledge is no different
from ethics. The logic of faith is the effort to unite what
is true and good with what is beautiful and just.

TERNARY LOGIC

Let us begin, therefore, with the turning point that the
emancipation of metaphysics from binary logic represented
in the twentieth century. For the Romanian-born French
philosopher Stéphane Lupasco (1900–1988), a close associate of Benjamin Fondane and a disciple of Shestov, the
affective should not be separated from the ontological, as
the whole of modern philosophy had claimed.[4] Stéphane
Lupasco did not reject the principle of non-contradiction,
but only its claim to be absolute. He was also influenced
by the work of the Austrian physicist Erwin Schrödinger
(1887–1961), one of the leading theoreticians of quantum
mechanics. As early as 1944, Schrödinger had conceived of
a thermodynamics of life. For him, living systems were to
be understood as self-replicating processes that maintained
themselves out of equilibrium by metabolizing the flow
of energy and matter that continuously passed through
them. The metabolism thus appeared to be fundamentally negentropic. Negentropy is defined as a factor in the
organization of physical, biological and potentially social

---

[4] B. Nicolescu manages to reconcile the different points of view
in the following way: "There can be no exclusive philosophy of
affectivity. Affectivity and the included third are in a relationship
of unity of contradictions. Affectivity without the included third
is just an empty word." B. Nicolescu, "The interrupted dialogue,"
chap. 9 in *What is Reality?* (Montréal: Liber Canada, 2009).

and human systems, opposing the natural tendency to disorganization (entropy). With the realization that everywhere in the universe self-organizing out-of-equilibrium systems were constantly being born and dying, natural and spontaneous production of negentropy (*autopoiesis*) appeared to be nature's answer to entropic death.

After studying the principles of entropy (the law of homogenization of matter) and negentropy (law of differentiation of living matter), Lupasco came to the conclusion that the relationships between objects within a system can no longer be based on the axioms of identity, non-contradiction and excluded third. Each state A is both A and not A to some degree. A permanent dynamic tension links them, and membership of one category or another (physical matter, living matter, conscious matter) is a question of the majority activation or potentiation of heterogeneity or homogeneity.

It was in his 1951 book, *The Principle of Antagonism and the Logic of Energy*, that Lupasco invented the principle of the included third, basing it on quantum mechanics. According to this axiom, there is a third term that is both A and not A, depending on the different levels of reality observed. In *Les trois matières*, a work published in 1970,[5] Lupasco showed that macrophysical matter obeys the laws of classical physics, while at the level of living matter, heterogenization is the dominant rule, and at the microphysical level, the forces of identity and non-identity are in equilibrium. At the latter level, the atomic energy depends on antagonistic tension. His logic is paradoxical: matter/antimatter, wave/particle, positive and negative electrons. Everything is in between actualization and reciprocal potentialization.

Basarab Nicolescu, a French physicist also of Romanian descent, and the founder of the Centre International de

---

[5] S. Lupasco, *Les trois matières* (Paris: Julliard, 1970).

Recherches et d'Études Transdisciplinaires (CIRET), was acquainted with Stéphane Lupasco. He claims that for Lupasco there are three different types of included third.

> *The logical included third* is useful in terms of the expansion of the class of phenomena that can be rationally understood. It explains the paradoxes of quantum mechanics, in their entirety, starting with the principle of super-position. More importantly, great discover-ies in the biology of consciousness are to be expected if mental barriers in relation to the notion of levels of Reality are to gradually dis-appear. This will show the fruitfulness of the *ontological included third*, implying the simulta-neous consideration of several levels of Reality. The third — the *secretly included third* — is the guardian of our irreducible mystery, the only possible basis for tolerance and human dignity. Without this third everything is ashes. Perhaps it was this third that Fondane was looking for, on the border between poetry, mysticism and philosophy. The secretly included third is the other name for affectivity.[6]

Basarab Nicolescu has deepened Lupasco's intuitions. For him, the levels of Reality and perception, included third, and complexity, define the methodology of trans-disciplinarity. They induce an isomorphism between the different domains of knowledge, thus determining a fractal structure of Reality.[7] The transdisciplinary method there-fore requires a change in the level of consciousness. The binary partition (subject, object), which defines modern metaphysics, is replaced, in the transdisciplinary approach, by the ternary partition (subject, object, hidden third). The third term, the hidden third, is reducible neither to the object nor to the subject. It allows us to think of the

---

[6] B. Nicolescu, "Le dialogue interrompu," in *Qu'est-ce que la réalité?*
[7] B. Nicolescu, *La transdisciplinarité* (Monaco: Éd. du Rocher, 1996).

"we" without reducing the You to the I (and vice versa), and to conceive the "he/they" in an inclusive way.

The revelation of the ternary character of human consciousness has implications for metaphysical representations of divinity in the East as well as in the West. For God is precisely the being who overcomes the opposition between potentiality and actuality. Thinkers as different as the agnostic philosopher Dany-Robert Dufour, in *Les Mystères de la trinité* (Paris: Gallimard, 1990) or the Orthodox Christian philosopher David Bentley Hart, already mentioned, have developed this aspect in depth:

> God is not a being who might and therefore must exist, but is absolute Being as such, apart from whom nothing else could exist, as either a possibility or an actuality. In God, logical possibility does not translate into logical necessity; it is instead God's necessity, as the unconditioned source of all things, that makes any world possible in the first place.[8]

Thanks to this understanding of the included third formed by the activity of consciousness, God can be understood (but not grasped) in the same way as the Fathers of the Church understood the term hypostasis. God self-reveals as infinite personal consciousness, identical to infinite being, in whom the ecstasy of the Spirit makes the fulfillment of accomplished knowledge correspond to created wisdom. There is therefore no longer any reason to bring monotheistic and cosmocentric traditions into opposition, even though both have different experiences of divinity and distinct levels of consciousness of ternarity. Nevertheless, ecumenical metaphysics makes the convergence of spiritual horizons possible through a sapiential personalism (point 2) and, to put it another way, through a personalistic sophiology (point 3).

---

[8] Hart, *The Experience of God*, 122.

SAPIENTIAL PERSONALISM

The history of the concept of person is very long-standing. Ancient philosophers understood the person as an individual consisting of soul and body. The Fathers of the Church showed that the judicial definition of the person as a non-object was not commensurate with the reality it denoted. For them, the person was to be understood as nothing more and nothing less than the image of God, an act of incarnation of truth. The whole question, from that point on, was to define the divine nature. Whilst Western thinkers such as Boethius and Thomas Aquinas considered this nature in the abstract, and therefore defined the person as "an individual substance of a rational nature," Eastern thinkers saw the divine nature as personal and therefore relational, but did not dare to penetrate the mystery of the divine "personhood."[9] From this difference in approach, which has become a flaw in ecumenical metaphysics, a third definition of the person as an ego appeared at the modern period, a transcendental I, distinct from the empirical self, which represents and speaks of self as a noun. The fourth definition of the person, in the contemporary era, known as "ontological-existential" by Emmanuel Housset, understands the person as "the being who receives his individuation from a call to alterity."

Spiritual metaphysics is based on a fifth, ecumenical conception of the person. It understands the person as a reality, therefore free, at once uncreated and created. It is important to remember here the limits of the phenomenological method mentioned earlier.[10] "There is, according to the philosopher Emmanuel Housset, an ipseity prior

---

[9] It should be noted that the term "personhood" is used by John Zizioulas to address the personal Trinitarian reality, and to avoid the anthropomorphism suggested by the term "personality."

[10] A. Arjakovsky, "Objectivation, subjectivation et transcendement: Michel Bitbol, Nicolas Berdyaev, Jean-Marc Ferry," in *Première, deuxième, troisième personne*, ed. N. Depraz (Bucharest: Zeta books, 2014), 322–34.

to egoity, there is a life that precedes the ability to say I."[11] Housset envisages an identity that is not based on transcendental reflection, but "on that which absolutely requires the self." However, this call remains confined to a reflective effort that is unable to fully awaken to the transcendent reality of Wisdom. Yet, as stated by Berdyaev, truth must be distinguished from objectivity:

> Truth does not enter us as an object. Truth implies the activity of man's spirit, the knowledge of truth depends on the degrees of community that can exist between men, on their communion in the Spirit.[12]

Similarly, Shestov, in one of his two articles on Husserl, summarized the main limitation of phenomenological thought for Russian religious philosophy as follows:

> Existential philosophy is not "reflection" (*Besinnung*), it does not question reality and does not seek truth in the immediate data of consciousness, but it strives to overcome what appears insurmountable in our thinking [...]. Possibilities are not determined by eternal truths that a dead hand has inscribed in the structure of being; they are in the power of a living, absolutely perfect being who created and blessed man. Whatever horrors and abominations we find in being [...] they in no way expose "the truth" in spite of the assurances of reason, they do not tell us that it is impossible to extricate them from being.[13]

The Swiss philosopher François-Xavier Putallaz, also aware of the limits of phenomenology, seeks to develop a metaphysics of the person. To him, a person is more than just a relationship or even a face. Indeed, Putallaz

---

[11] E. Housset, *La différence personnelle, Essai sur l'identité dramatique de la personne humaine* (Paris: Hermann, 2019), 173.

[12] N. Berdyaev, *Cinq méditations sur l'existence* (Paris: Aubier, 1936), 203.

[13] L. Chestov, "À la mémoire d'un grand philosophe Edmund Husserl," in *Spéculation et révélation* (Paris: L'Âge d'Homme, 1981), 218.

defined the person as "a concrete subject, individual, and incommunicable existing inside a human nature that is communicable to all members of the species."[14] This definition has the advantage of including any person who is not always capable of communicating the properties that characterize humanity, whether it is a newborn baby or an Alzheimer's sufferer. However, as will become apparent, one can wonder about the boundaries of such a definition that is content to distinguish between the order of existence and the order of essence.

It is indeed a question of approaching the mystery of the person through a sapiential understanding of being, made of permanence and unpredictability due to the magnetization of Wisdom created by divine Wisdom, and its dynamic of openness and incarnation, on account of its own freedom and its relational character. Ecumenical metaphysics thus understands man as a person, a microcosm and a macrocosm, as a being who is both individual and connected, who flourishes through and for others in the name of the common good. "The person," writes Berdyaev, "is created by God's idea and man's freedom."[15]

However, this approach is not only theological, it is also philosophical. For an understanding of this, it is necessary to go back to the metaphysical debate over universals during the medieval period. Nicolas Berdyaev dates this dispute to the time when reason and faith cease to agree. According to the Russian philosopher, the great problem, which undermined Western philosophy, was how to define reality.[16]

For realists (universalists), *universalia sunt realia*. Universals are really things, realities that exist outside the

---

[14] F.-X. Putallaz, "Pour une métaphysique de la personne," in *L'humain et la personne*, ed. Putallaz and Bernard N. Schumacher (Paris: Éd. du Cerf, 2008), 316.

[15] N. Berdyaev, *De la destination de l'homme* (Paris: Je sers, 1935), 80.

[16] N. Berdyaev, *Essai de métaphysique eschatologique* (Paris: Aubier, 1946), 140.

human mind. The product of thought is denied in things: this is the result of objectification. For the conceptualists, *universalia in re*, the concept is in the individual thing itself. Universals are therefore concepts, mental constructions. It is a lower degree of objectification, but it remains an abstract thought that leads to pantheism. Indeed, for Spinoza, God does not love individuals, only eternal essences. This is where the nominalists have innovated. For William of Ockham, *universalia sunt post rem*. Thought is recognized as dependent on the world of objects. For the Franciscan theologian, universals are mere words. It was a reaction to the realism of concepts. However, it led to the denial of the reality of the individual.

In his *Essay on Eschatological Metaphysics*, Berdyaev explains that the confusion at the origin of this dispute was already present in Plato and Aristotle. The Greek philosophers started with deduction from the general to the particular, from the species to the individual. In short, they confused the universal and the general. From then on, universals dominated the individual but were devoid of concrete existence. For Berdyaev, the universal is not at all the general. It is not a product of abstract thought and is not opposed to the individual: the universal raises the individual to the fullness of existential substance. While the general is abstract, God, as a person, is the highest universal and the most concrete individual.[17] At this particular level, the universal is understood as a category that is both personal and sapiential, that is to say, ecumenical.

Thus Berdyaev distanced himself from the universalism of Hegel, from the concrete universal, but also from all conceptualism (the source of rationalism) and nominalism

---

[17] "The concept is common and abstract, and to the concept the common and abstract is the primary reality, while the individual acquires a secondary, derivative significance. This view is characteristic of objectifying thought," ibid., 141. N. Berdyaev, *The Beginning and the End*, part 2, chap. 4, 119.

(which admits no concrete form). According to Berdyaev,
ecumenical metaphysics is personalistic. "According to existential personalism, the universal exists, but it exists as a
qualification of personality."[18] It overcomes the closed character of individual consciousness as conceived by empir-
icism. The ontological method of deducing truth from
the concept of the object is thus abandoned. Berdyaev
therefore joins Heidegger's critique of ontotheology. For
the Russian philosopher, ontologism reveals the posthu-
mous victory of Abelard, not the primacy of being but
that of the concept.

> As opposed to Platonism and scholastic realism,
> as opposed to all forms of rationalism, what is
> true is not that the world of the senses is indi-
> vidual and unique, while the world of ideas, the
> noumenal world is the world of the common and
> the universal; the truth is that in the phenom-
> enal world of the senses everything is brought
> into subjection to the common, to the species, to
> law, whereas in the noumenal world everything
> is individual and personal.[19]

PERSONALIST SOPHIOLOGY

The philosopher Nicolas Berdyaev, in his commentary
on the *Mysterium magnum* of Jakob Boehme, identified
Wisdom with the deepest freedom of God and man. Like
Sergius Bulgakov, he was at the same time permeated by
the insights of the German mystic, and the need to bring
rationality to the volcanic nature of this thought.[20] For
his part, Father Bulgakov shared the same metaphysical
concept of the person as his friend Nicolas Berdyaev. His

---

[18] N. Berdyaev, *Essai de métaphysique eschatologique*, 142; ibid., par. 120.
[19] Ibid., 143; ibid., par. 121.
[20] A. Arjakovsky, *La Génération des penseurs religieux de l'émigra-
tion russe* (Paris: L'Esprit et la Lettre, 2002); A. Arjakovsky, *The
Way: Religious Thinkers of the Religious Emigration in Paris and
their Journal, 1925–1940* (South Bend, IN: University of Notre
Dame Press, 2013).

contribution consisted in clarifying this from a theological rather than philosophical point of view. He defined the person of the Father in a personalist, sophiological and ternary manner:

> The Father is Sophia (but, of course, not vice versa). This equality expresses the idea that, insofar as Sophia is objective, divine self- revelation, she reveals and expresses the hidden essence of the Father; she is His genuine predicate, whose true Subject He is. Sophia, as Divine-humanity, belongs to the Father; she is His revelation. In this sense, the Father is Divine-humanity; however, He is the Divine-humanity which is not manifested, which is hidden and mysterious, but which is becoming manifested in divine self-revelation. The Divine-humanity is the manifested countenance of the Father. It is the Mystery of the Father, hidden in Him, but manifested by the Revealing hypostases.[21]

This sapiential representation of the personhood of God, also rediscovered by Catholic ecumenists such as Father Marie Joseph Le Guillou, has, of course, implications for the conception of the human person. Personal consciousness does not manifest itself in a closed self. The "I" postulates and presupposes a "you," "him," and "us."

> In creaturely, relative being, I is posited not only in itself but also outside itself; it is extrapolated and thereby limited. Despite its seeming absoluteness, I is not capable of actualising its I-ness in itself and must, so to speak, become convinced of its own being by looking into the mirror of other I's. Without such a mirror, it disappears for itself, stops being conscious of itself in its I-ness.[22]

---

[21] S. Bulgakov, *Le Paraclet* (Paris: L'Âge d'Homme, 1996), 349; S. Bulgakov, *The Comforter* (Grand Rapids, MI: Wm. B. Eerdmans Publishing Co., 2004), 366.

[22] Ibid., 62; ibid., 54.

In order to understand this crucial development in theology, and therefore in anthropology, it is necessary to return to the evolution of sophiological thought in the twentieth century. By redefining the concept of the person in a sapiential way, Bulgakov also gave new meaning to the categories used to describe the Trinitarian life. The clarification by the Vatican that the doctrine of the *filioque* must not lead to a subordination of the person of the Holy Spirit in the Trinity, dates only from 1995.[23]

Until recently, Orthodox theology, in the confessional sense of the term, contested the Catholic understanding that "persons" "appear" as "accidents" within the divine life. It was not until the ecumenical renewal of Christian theology in the twentieth century that it became clear that the use of Neoplatonic categories could not be adequate for the definition of "divine personhood," as expressed by John Zizioulas.

Briefly stated,[24] sophiology worked in the twentieth century on four intuitions of patristic theology, in particular the notions of love, person, *kenosis* (of self-emptying) or *perichoresis* (of circumincession) of the Trinitarian *hypostases*, to arrive at four original theological opinions.

Firstly, the unity of God resides in the Person of the Father and not in an impersonal divine substance. Secondly, the Christian Trinity is not the mere juxtaposition of three distinct self-consciousnesses, united only externally. The divine personhood is a tri-unity which has, in

---

[23] Dicastère pour la promotion de l'unité des Chrétiens, "Les traditions grecque et latine concernant la procession du Saint-Esprit," *Documentation Catholique* 19 (Paris, September 13, 1995), 941–45. Dicastery for Promoting Christian Unity, "The Greek and Latin Traditions Regarding the Procession of the Holy Spirit," 1987. www.christianunity.va/content/unitacristiani/en/documenti/altri-testi/en1.html (last accessed August 5, 2025).

[24] See A. Arjakovsky, *Le père Serge Boulgakov, philosophe et théologien chrétien* (Paris: Parole et Silence, 2006).

Trinitarianism, the fullness and power of its being. Thirdly, the personalist and sapiential metaphysics allows for an understanding of the "procession" of the Holy Spirit, but not as a causal relationship or as a generation.

Personalist sophiology prefers to use the category of "divine tri-hypostatic aseity," i.e. "the existence of and from the self of the triune God." It also employs the logic of the included third to show that the hypostasis, or self-consciousness, can be, through the notion of self-revelation, both identical and distinct from its sapiential nature.[25] Divine Wisdom in fact reveals the double unity of the Son and the Spirit, a unique revelation of the Father. Trinitarian life must therefore be understood in a personalist, sapiential and ternary manner.

Bulgakov uses a whole range of arguments for his purposes. The exegetical argument is probably the one that has had the most impact on theology of the twentieth century.[26] Indeed, in Luke's Gospel, Christ, the One anointed with the Spirit, reveals that the Spirit of the Lord is upon him (Lk 4:18). The Spirit *rests* on the Son. This is why Bulgakov defines the divine Spirit in this way:

> The divine spirit, spirit of the Father and spirit of the Son, is the Holy Spirit, who is not only the Holy Spirit and the Third Hypostasis, but who is also the Spirit of God [...]. The Holy Spirit exists by the virtue of the Father and the Son as Their mutual love and as the Love of Themselves.[27]

It is Wisdom that allows such an understanding. Ecumenical science revives the notion of Wisdom, not only as a virtue, which it has all too often been reduced to, but

---

[25] S. Boulgakov, *Le Paraclet*, 132; S. Bulgakov, *The Comforter*, 138.
[26] B. Bobrinskoy, *La Compassion du Père* (Paris: Éd. du Cerf, 2000); see also the article by E. Behr Sigel, "La sophiologie du père Serge Boulgakoff," *Revue d'histoire et de philosophie religieuses*, 19.2 (1939), 130–58.
[27] Ibid., 146.

in its dual created and uncreated form, as the innermost
life of the being. It can neither be reduced to being—
since, according to biblical revelation, it penetrates all
spirits[28]— nor can it be identified with a single person
of the Divine Being.[29] According to Bulgakov:

> Thus, God's being is the supra-eternal act of the
> Trinity's self-affirmation, realized in Sophia [...].
> God's self-revelation in the Divine Sophia, or
> the divine world, is a perfect and adequate act
> of divinity's life, which is nonhypostatic ("natu-
> ral") in its own content but trihypostatic in its
> procession and self-affirmation.[30]

This conception of being as wisdom allows truth to
be understood neither as an autonomous and stable
mathematical law, which characterizes modern thought,
nor as a permanently evolving structure and devoid of
levels, which is the mark of postmodern philosophy. The
truth, for ecumenical science, is found in the tension
between the gift of the creative purpose in history and

---

[28] Ws 7:22–30: "For in her there is a spirit that is intelligent,
holy, unique, manifold, subtle, mobile, clear, unpolluted, distinct,
invulnerable, loving the good, keen, irresistible, beneficent, humane,
steadfast, sure, free from anxiety, all powerful, overseeing all, and
penetrating through all spirits that are intelligent and pure and
most subtle. For wisdom is more mobile than any motion; because
of her pureness she pervades and penetrates all things. For she is
a breath of the power of God, and a pure emanation of the glory
of the Almighty; therefore, nothing defiled gains entrance into her.
For she is a reflection of eternal light, a spotless mirror of the
working of God, and an image of his goodness. Though she is
but one, she can do all things, and while remaining in herself, she
renews all things; in every generation she passes into holy souls
and makes them friends of God, and prophets; for God loves
nothing so much as the man who lives with wisdom. For she is
more beautiful than the sun, and excels every constellation of the
stars. Compared with the light she is found to be superior, for it is
succeeded by the night, but against wisdom evil does not prevail."
[29] A. Arjakovsky, *Essai sur le père Serge Boulgakov, philosophe et
théologien chrétien* (Paris: Parole et Silence, 2006).
[30] S. Boulgakov, *L'Épouse de l'Agneau*, 40; S. Bulgakov, *The Bride
of the Lamb*, 43.

the celebration of its unveiling, the personal quest for moral righteousness and the communal concern for the fulfillment of justice.

The discourse on Wisdom is a metaphysics of love insofar as Wisdom is both beyond and in the midst of phenomena. The sense by which the person is measured is that of divine-humanity, the incarnation of God in man and the assumption of man in God. This is the reason why human rationality must be able to associate intelligence of a symbolic type, uniting nature and culture, with the conceptual mode of knowledge. The philosopher Jean Borella has shown the limits of modern agnostic rationalism in its materialist version as well as in the so-called Christian theology of the modern and confessional age. For him, human rationality is necessarily open and therefore ternary, capable, for those who know how to allow themselves, of associating a referent to any signified and to any signifier. Here he joins Heidegger when the latter invites man to open his ear "to the silent voice of being that speaks to his essence, so that he may learn to experience Being in the Nothing." This ecumenical metaphysics thus gives considerable space to language as an expression and vehicle of the meeting of created and uncreated Wisdom in the Spirit. By its universal character, both personal and spiritual, Wisdom is the foundation of ecumenical metaphysics. As such, sophiology is also a reflection on the developing unity of the Churches, and, beyond that, on the paths to convergence of different religious and convictional traditions. This is what Father Sergius Bulgakov has to say in his summary of sophiology:

> What do we mean by the reunion of the churches in one Church? Is this a "pact" or an act that is a manifestation of the one Church as a revelation of Divine-humanity, as Sophia the Wisdom of God? Until the consciousness of the Church can reach this depth of self-determination, all

ecumenical pacts will be in vain. Again and
again will the separated churches dash in vain
against the walls which divide them, in a tragic
realization of their helplessness, in face of the
objective impossibility of genuine reunion. There
is, nevertheless, one true way, which is that of
learning to know and understand the Church as
revealed Divine humanity, Sophia the Wisdom
of God.[31]

For Jews, Christians and Muslims, the biblical figure
of Wisdom is universal. As the book of Proverbs reveals,
it is addressed not to a particular group of believers, but
to "all the sons of Adam." It is both penetrating and pen-
etrated intellect, which makes it possible to give rational
expression to faith, and to connect rationality with spirit.

Although the cultural worlds are very different, Chinese
thought comes close to this experience of Wisdom as the
deepest dimension of the world in its understanding of
the relationship between Yin and Yang. François Cheng
has explained what is meant by the notion of *shen-yu* or
"divine resonance" which participates in the whole organization of living things:

> *Shen* embodies the superior state of *qi*, "Breath":
> it is generally translated as the spirit or the
> divine spirit. Just like *qi*, *shen* is at the founda-
> tion of the living universe. Whereas, according to
> Chinese thought, the primordial Breath animates
> all forms of life, the Spirit, for its part, governs
> the mental part, the conscious part of the living
> universe. This conception may surprise. To say
> that man, as a thinking being, is inhabited by
> *shen* seems acceptable to everyone. But on the
> other hand, to affirm that the universe itself is
> inhabited by *shen* as well, and that, most impor-
> tantly, it is governed by it, can appear suspect

---

[31] S. Boulgakov, *La Sagesse de Dieu, Résumé de sophiologie* (Paris:
L'Âge d'Homme, 1983 [1936]), 16; S. Bulgakov, *The Wisdom of God,
An Outline of Sophiology* (New York: Lindisfarne Press, 1993), 19.

to a pure materialist. The deep reason for such
a conception is that Chinese thought does not
separate matter and spirit. It reasons in terms
of life, which is the basic unit. It distinguishes
levels in the order of life but does not recognize
discontinuities, organic ruptures between them.[32]

This metaphysical evolution has far-reaching implications for our understanding of reality and the knowledge
that allows us to access it. At the same time that mediaeval
metaphysics developed, with the founding of universities in
Bologna and Paris, the teaching of the *trivium* and *quadrivium*, idealist metaphysics established a new epistemology
based on philosophy— since the University, according to
Schelling, had to institutionalize the systematic requirement of philosophy: to account for the unity of the totality— the principles of ecumenical metaphysics today forge
a new conception of the organization of knowledge that
it is now a question of presenting.

---

[32] F. Cheng, *Cinq méditations sur la beauté* (Paris: Albin Michel,
2006).

4

The Ecumenical Understanding of Science

ECUMENICAL metaphysics is the foundation of a new understanding of reality, of a new epistemology, both trans-disciplinary and trans-confessional but also trans-religious and trans-convictional; it consists in rediscovering the ties in tension that unite human beings to reality, according to distinct levels of consciousness. In particular, this epistemology allows us to reconcile two ancient conceptions of truth, namely the *doxa* or personal opinion (when it is true, or right, or faithful, or just) and the *episteme* or shared conviction (when it is analogical, or coherent, or consensual, or enduring). It also reconciles two representations, the Jewish and the Greek, of the very act of knowledge: as the fruit of an interpersonal encounter that is certain (*emeth*) and as the self-disclosure of being (*aletheia*).

CRITIQUE OF THE SCIENTISTIC VIEW OF SCIENCE

In order to understand this approach, it is necessary to remember that science, as we define it today, is a recent invention. As Georges Gusdorf has shown, what we mean today by science is a viewpoint that is less than two hundred years old.[1] Originally, for Émile Littré, the word science, in Greek *episteme*, in Latin *scientia*, simply meant the knowledge that one has of something. Until the seventeenth century, the sciences were integrated into the liberal arts. These could be taught insofar as they allowed freedom of thought. General culture included the literary disciplines (*trivium*) of grammar, rhetoric, dialectics

---

[1] G. Gusdorf, *De l'histoire des sciences à l'histoire de la pensée* (Paris: Payot, 1966).

and the scientific disciplines (*quadrivium*) of arithmetic, geometry, astronomy and music. According to Scholasticism, the heir to Hellenic thought, the importance of science was recognized by the value of its subject. This is why it culminated in Metaphysics, considered to be the queen of sciences. The highest knowledge was that of supreme reality. It was therefore of an ontological and theological nature. The human mind, in order to flourish, had to receive the revelation of a truth that transcends it, interpret it with the help of *disputatio* to determine its meaning, apply its teachings to the real world (notably through medicine) and codify them (in law).

Modern thought is characterized by a shift in the idea of science which, increasingly in the age of Enlightenment, concerns the *form* rather than the *content* of knowledge. In the eighteenth century, philosophers such as Christian Wolff defined science as the practice of demonstrating what one asserts, i.e., deducing it from certain and unchangeable principles by way of legitimate inference. The idea of science has moved from a project of unveiling essences to that of ordering phenomena, due in particular to the pressure of inductive methodologies and positivism. As a result, the modern university was no longer able to admit that the same thinker, Descartes or Leibniz, author of philosophical essays on the one hand and mathematical treatises on the other, could be considered as a man of letters and therefore of science. Today, according to Gusdorf:

> Only statements that correspond to experimental protocols have real meaning, those that can be verified according to the ways and means of the laboratory. In the eyes of the latest proponents of scientism, the formulas of the theologian or the metaphysician have no more validity than those of the poet.[2]

---

[2] Ibid., 20.

Many people today believe that trying to save the notion and name of science is futile due to the technical sophistication of scientific reasoning. For us, on the other hand, science, understood as authentic knowledge, is a human effort to conceptualize and symbolize an object of knowledge determined through the personal, sapiential and ternary experience of being, understood as signifier, signified and referent. To do this, it follows a precise and adapted method, coherent and open. It is able to justify this method in its own eyes and in the eyes of any person willing to commit to working towards this objective and following this method.

From this perspective, ecumenical metaphysics is the search for a universal wisdom capable of providing human beings with a spiritual and comprehensive understanding of the world, humankind, and God through a participatory process of openness, reflection, enquiry, dialogue, judgment, and collaboration. Its unique methodology enables the definition of various levels of awareness and participation in reality. Based on the transdisciplinary concept of consciousness, it seeks to bring together the polarities of the beautiful, the true, the good, and the just.

Ecumenical metaphysics is primarily the result of the slow decay of scientism in contemporary times. Scientism is the ideology according to which all problems concerning humanity and the world can best be solved by following the paradigm of a so-called scientific method which, on the one hand, radically distinguishes the thinking subject from extended matter and, on the other hand, ignores the participatory dimension of knowledge in the making of reality. As will be seen later, this scientistic ideology has its origins in Cartesian dualism. It culminates in Auguste Comte's "law of three states," as well as in a number of reductionist thoughts such as *diamat* (dialectical materialism) and *histmat* (historical materialism). Scientistic epistemology, now prominent in universities and government departments, ranges from biology to psychology, and from political science to economic science. It is based on the belief that "knowing is believing." This ideology is particularly strong in the transhumanist nebula and within the *Singularity University*.[3] Since Francis Bacon, its scientific cleric, it has had its own conception of salvation and intangible dogmas. One of them postulates that unconscious matter constitutes the only reality. Nature is a machine; it has no intention, and its laws are immutable. According to this belief, human consciousness is nothing but brain activity. The notion of freedom is swept away by that of determinism. This rationalism has led, in the words of Charles Taylor, to the "malaise of modernity" marked by three main phenomena: The fading of moral horizons; the eclipse of ends in the face of rampant instrumental reason; and the loss of freedom.[4]

For more than a century, however, this powerful gnosis has been gradually challenged. The main arguments advanced by biologist Rupert Sheldrake, as well as physicists Basarab Nicolescu and John Polkinghorne, against scientism are the following. The universe is more like a cloud than a clock. This observation requires us to recognize that nature, through creative evolution, forms entities larger than the sum of their parts, leading us to embrace a holistic view of the universe, as a unifying and totalizing synthesis at work from the atom to the personality of man. The theory of constant conservation of energy in the universe and the law of entropy should not be dogmatized, given the negentropic forces observed in living organisms, and the vast amount of dark matter that constitutes the universe. For R. Sheldrake, "the appearance of matter and energy should not be confined to the very first instant, as

---

[3] A. Lécu, B. de Malherbe, D. Folsheid, *Le Transhumanisme, c'est quoi?* (Paris: Éd. du Cerf, 2018).

[4] C. Taylor, *Le Malaise de la modernité* (Paris: Éd. du Cerf, 2002); *The Malaise of Modernity* (Toronto, House of Anansi Press, 2024).

in the standard Big Bang theory. Rather, the universe is more like an organism expanding because of dark energy and creating more dark energy by expanding."[5] The flow of energy could also depend on how the body is connected to a larger flow of energy present in all of nature.

> Terms like spirit, prana and chi may refer to a kind of energy that mechanistic science has missed out but which would show up quantitatively through discrepancies in calorimeter studies.[6]

As the physicist and Christian theologian François Euvé has stated, there was a shift in perception at the beginning of the revolution brought about by quantum physics. God is not powerless, as moderns believed; God is not omnipotent in the sense of being coercive, but in his ability to stir free and creative beings, rather than obedient and servile machines. Speaking with purpose does not necessarily imply constraint. God's plan is played out in history according to the loving relationship between God and man. God is not a clockmaker, not even a brilliant one, as Newton thought. He is more like a lover who invites his beloved to participate in his work:

> The marital model is biblically more accurate than the workmanship model. Rather than a God who makes a world, with everything else appearing as objects for Him to use, He is a God who makes a covenant with His creation, especially humanity.[7]

---

[5] R. Sheldrake, *Réenchanter la science* (Paris: J'ai lu, 2016); R. Sheldrake, *The Science Delusion: Freeing the Spirit of Enquiry* (London: Coronet, 2020).

[6] Ibid., 142; ibid., 84.

[7] These axioms of quantum physics can be summarized as follows: Non-separability: in the quantum world two entities are always connected regardless of distance; Indeterminism: the quantum world is neither wave nor particle: it is both that and that — this is the logic of the included third (logic of the excluded third: either that or that); Quantum superposition: and yes and no;

A TRANSDISCIPLINARY EPISTEMOLOGY

The stakes in the critique of scientism are high because it is the very future of contemporary civilization, threatened in particular by transhumanist utopianism, which is at stake:

> As the prefix "trans" indicates, transdisciplinarity concerns that which is at once between the disciplines, across the different disciplines, and beyond all discipline. Its goal is the understanding of the present world, of which one of the imperatives is the unity of knowledge.
>
> Is there something between and across disciplines and beyond all disciplines? From the point of view of classical thought there is absolutely nothing. The space in question is empty, completely void, like the vacuum of classical physics. Even if it renounces the pyramidal vision of knowledge, classical thought considers each fragment of the pyramid which is generated by the disciplinary big bang as an entire pyramid; each discipline claims that it is sufficient unto itself. For classical thought transdisciplinarity appears absurd because it does not appear to have an object. In contrast, within the framework of transdisciplinarity, classical thought does not appear absurd; rather, it simply appears to have a restricted sphere of applicability.
>
> In the presence of several levels of Reality the space between disciplines and beyond disciplines is full, just as the quantum void is full of all potentialities — from the quantum particle to the galaxies, from the quark to the heavy elements that condition the appearance of life in the universe.[8]

---

in a richer world a cylinder can be square or round. The usual space-time is an anthropomorphic construction: space is abstract in the quantum world; Incompleteness of physical laws: Gödel's theorems (1931) — one can never derive all possible results from an experiment: you can have yes and no.

[8] B. Nicolescu, *La Transdisciplinarité*, xxvii; B. Nicolescu,

From a transdisciplinary perspective, knowledge is ternary and therefore antinomic. It is also oriented towards a finality which is eschatological, in the sense that it does not include the finality of things in a merely horizontal way, absorbed in time. At the same time, it is vertical and interpersonal, since truth has an existential dimension. When it is connected, human intelligence is able to grasp the loops of coherence that constitute reality. Ecumenical thinking is therefore based on the method of transdisciplinarity, in order to think together unity and plurality in the simultaneous consideration of several levels of reality and their corresponding levels of consciousness:

> A new *Principle of Relativity* emerges from the coexistence between complex plurality and open unity: *no one level of Reality constitutes a privileged place from which one is able to understand all the other levels of Reality.* A level of Reality is what it is because all the other levels exist at the same time. This Principle of Relativity is what originates a new perspective on religion, politics, art, education, and social life. In the transdisciplinary vision, Reality is not only multi-dimensional, it is also multi-referential. The different levels of Reality are accessible to human knowledge thanks to the existence of different *levels of perception,* which are in bi-univocal correspondence with levels of Reality. These levels of perception permit an increasingly general, unifying, encompassing vision of Reality, without ever entirely exhausting it. As in the case of levels of Reality the coherence of levels of perception presupposes a zone of *non-resistance* to perception. The unity of levels of perception and its complementary zone of non-resistance constitutes *the transdisciplinary Subject.*[9]

Transdisciplinarity: Theory and Practice (Cresskill, NJ: Hampton Press, 2008), 2–3.
[9] Ibid., 9.

The Orthodox Christian thinker, Basarab Nicolescu, gives the key to the intimate link between transdisciplinarity and ecumenical science. In the transdisciplinary vision, complex plurality and open unity are two sides of the same Reality. The structure of all the levels of Reality is a complex structure: each level is what it is because all the other levels exist at the same time.

Ecumenical metaphysics is based on a trans-disciplinary methodology. This thinking is both holistic and complex, as with Edgar Morin, but through its openness to the Spirit, it is also capable of finding a coherence between noumena and phenomena. By drawing on the spiritual and metaphysical traditions of the East and the West, it associates the Western openness to transcendence (which has incorporated all the Nietzschean and Jewish critique of idols) with the Eastern sense of harmony (which, like François Cheng, has included the sense of the mystery of the human face). Ecumenical epistemology is thus the result of interaction between the person (divine or human), consciousness (cosmic or personal) and reality (created or uncreated). Its representation of consciousness has, because of its relationship with the created or uncreated Wisdom, an ethical depth. This depth was brought to light by François Rabelais, in 1534, in the dialogue between Gargantua and his son Pantagruel:

> But because, according to Solomon the Wise, wisdom does not enter into an ill-disposed soul, and science without conscience is but the ruin of the soul — it behoves you to serve, love, and fear God, and in Him put all your thoughts and all your hope; and by faith formed of charity, be adjoined to Him, in such wise that you never be sundered from Him by sin. Hold suspect the abuses of the world; set your heart not on vanity, for this life is transitory, but the word of God abides eternally. Be helpful to all your neighbours, and love them as yourself. Reverence your tutors.

Shun the company of those you do not want to
resemble; and as for the graces that God has
granted you, these do not receive in vain.[10]

TRANS-DISCIPLINARY EPISTEMOLOGY RENEWS CONFESSIONAL EPISTEMOLOGY

The overcoming of modern rationality has been accompanied by a new, eschatological, symbolic and antinomical
conception of the Church. The Church is now understood
not only institutionally as the "Body of Christ" (its dominant meaning in the West from the Council of Trent
onwards), but also, more mystically and universally, as
the "Bride of the Lamb" (a definition found in John's book
of Revelation, and updated in the twentieth century by
theologians such as Cardinal Marc Ouellet).

Similarly, the new epistemology presents itself as
trans-confessional, trans-religious and trans-convictional,
in that it is concerned with all experiences that lead to
the unification of consciousness, from Zoroastrianism to
Christianity, from Shamanism to Taoism. This ecumenical
dimension of epistemology is not, however, syncretistic.
It is characterized by its rigorous respect for the levels
of consciousness and the specific worlds of the different
environments under study. Its objective is to highlight
the specificities of each tradition. It knows what it owes
to Christian metaphysics, notably its conception of the
divinity of the person, and its Trinitarian understanding
of Wisdom. It does not neglect, however, the contribution of Judaism and Islam, with their ethical and unified
conception of divinity, nor that of Eastern philosophies,
with their sense of sapiential harmony in tension, and
their ternary conception of divinity.

---

[10] F. Rabelais, *Les cinq livres des faits et dits de Gargantua et Pantagruel* (Paris: Gallimard, 2017), chap. 8; Rabelais, "How Pantagruel,
while in Paris, received a Letter from his Father Gargantua, and
a Copy of the Same." In *The Complete Works of François Rabelais*,
Book 2, chap. 8 (London: Global Grey, 2020), 162.

Ecumenical metaphysics can be classed as a science if it produces results that are coherent (but not necessarily homogeneous), verifiable (but not necessarily falsifiable), predictable (but not always guaranteed) and universal (in the hyper-realistic sense, that is, respecting personal levels of consciousness). This ecumenical thought does not require immediate adherence. It is necessary to depart from the modern rationalist *a priori* according to which only the perception of visible phenomena necessarily produces knowledge. It is better to return to the medieval conception of degrees of knowledge varying according to the quality of interpersonal relations. This was basically Pascal's view of the orders of knowledge, with the difference that he did not imagine the dynamics of the relationships existing from one level of consciousness to another. This new rationality is called ecumenical insofar as it is capable of uniting in diversity, of thinking together the subject and the object, the good and the just, the true and the beautiful, religious and agnostic thoughts. Against ultra-specialized thought, which atrophies the sense of synthesis of consciousness, ecumenical thought associates concepts with levels of participation in reality.

This approach has a significant double effect. It enables us to move away from the heavily prevalent secularized conception of religion at universities. On the one hand, "rationalists" reject the religious approach, both critical and symbolic, of the desacralization of idols and plural unification of human diversity in connection with a transcendent, supernatural referent. On the other hand, "fideists," who are most often adherents of secularism understood as a civil religion, have a tendency to confuse their own convictions with the truth.

The result of this situation, which stems from a general opposition to the existing links between faith and reason, is that "belief" is systematically opposed to "knowledge." Yet modern sociology's distinction between believing and knowing is a very long-standing one and must be challenged, according to Eric Vinson.

> Yes, mature human sciences must not ignore the significance of the phenomena of belief, or at least of opinion, within "knowledge" itself; nor ignore anthropological "knowledge" — or should we say wisdom? — (existential, ethical, even metaphysical, in any case often strictly intellectual) conveyed by traditions, yet conveniently placed on the side of a devalued "belief."[11]

Ecumenical metaphysics grasps religious experience in all its complexity and depth, personally and socially, pluralistically and universally, theologically and philosophically, historically and meta-historically. To counter the fear of proselytism of agnostic scholars and the fear of relativism of religious scholars, ecumenical science proposes a method that is both comprehensive and comparative with regard to religious experiences. It promotes a transdisciplinary approach capable of preserving a relational and holistic worldview, characteristic of mystical experience, while mobilizing the tools and resources of different disciplines in an attempt to give meaning (orientation, significance, sensibility).

The dialogic method has been theorized by Hans-Georg Gadamer,[12] Jean-Marc Ferry,[13] Francis Jacques,[14] Jill Tabart.[15] It is based on respect for different levels of

---

[11] "For a science of religion. To know and teach religious fact in a secular framework: a challenge primarily epistemological and academic?" in Eric Vinson, *La science des religions* (Paris: Que sais-je?, 2019).

[12] H.-G, Gadamer, *Vérité et méthode* (Paris: Points, 2018); H.G. Gadamer, *Truth and Method*, trans. Garrett Bowden and John Cumming (New York: Seabury Press, 1975).

[13] J.-M. Ferry, *La Religion réflexive* (Paris: Éd. du Cerf, 2010).

[14] F. Jacques, *Dans l'ordre du cœur, Du paradoxe à la parabole* (Paris: Éd. du Cerf, 2019).

[15] J. Tabart, *Coming to consensus: a case study for the churches* (Geneva: WCC, 2003).

consciousness, on the translation of discourses, on the search for consensus, and on the transformation from conceptual rationality to open rationality, or, according to the expression of F. Jacques, on the passage "from paradox to parable." This science of the Spirit incorporates the classical requirement of coherence between the cosmic order, the political world, and personal experience. It recognizes the modern concern for freedom of conscience through the enhancement of critical thinking; it shares the postmodern desire for recognition of the uniqueness of persons in all their diversity. In line with the advances of contemporary science, ecumenical metaphysics proposes a new relation to space-time through an integral approach to reality.

Furthermore, ecumenical metaphysics releases the current teaching of "ecumenical studies" from the often, narrow approach of confessional ecclesiologies. Churches tend to reduce the universality of the Church to their own conceptions of the universal, which often leads to contradictory positions.

Thus, for example, the Orthodox Church affirmed, at its Kolymbari Council in 2016, its firm commitment to the ecumenical movement. However, four years later, a theological commission of the Ecumenical Patriarchate stated unequivocally that the Orthodox Church "understands itself" as the universal Church.

> §50 The Orthodox Church understands herself to be the one, holy, catholic, and apostolic Church, of which the Nicene-Constantinopolitan symbol of faith speaks. It is the Church of the Councils, continuous in charism and commission from the time of the Apostolic Council in Jerusalem (Acts 15:5–29) up to the present day. It lacks nothing essential to the full catholicity and full unity of the body of Christ, and possesses the fullness of all sacramental, magisterial, and pastoral grace. As Fr. Georges Florovsky wrote: "The Orthodox are bound to claim that the only

'specific' or 'distinctive' feature about their own position in 'divided Christendom' is the fact that the Orthodox Church is essentially identical with the Church of all ages, and indeed with the 'Early Church.' In other words, it is not *a* Church, but *the* Church. It is a formidable, but a fair and a just claim. There is here more than just an unbroken *historic continuity*, which is indeed quite obvious. There is above all an ultimate *spiritual and ontological identity*, the same faith, the same spirit, the same ethos. And this constitutes the distinctive mark of Orthodoxy. 'This is the Apostolic faith, this is the faith of the Fathers, this is the Orthodox faith, this faith has established the universe.'"[16]

On reading this text, one wonders whether the Orthodox Church has not returned to the time when the ecumenical movement was understood only as a place of mission, since it lacks "nothing essential" to its full catholicity. It is as if the authors of the text, but also the Ecumenical Patriarch Bartholomew, who congratulated the authors, had not noticed the divisions affecting not only the universal Church but also the Orthodox Church. We know that, since 2014, a war has been tearing two nations apart, Russia and Ukraine, both of which have a Christian Orthodox majority, and that, since 2018, a break in communion has occurred between the seats of Moscow and Constantinople...

The blindness of confessional consciousness, based on the sole understanding of orthodoxy as faithful memory, only reinforces our point. Only the new configuration of relations between faith and reason offered by ecumenical metaphysics allows the Churches to rethink adequately and justly their ecclesiology as well as their authentic

---

[16] *For the Life of the World: Towards a Social Ethos of the Orthodox Church*, Social Ethos Preface — Greek Orthodox Archdiocese of America (www.goarch.org) (last accessed August 6, 2025).

participation in the one, holy, catholic and apostolic Church. It also helps them humbly to acknowledge the wounds that affect the whole body of the Church, without losing their faith in the coming of the Kingdom of God on earth, and in their mission in the preparation for this sacrament. Notably, the new trans-disciplinary and trans-faith/religious/convictional epistemology has developed over the centuries a number of methods that now need to be presented.

5

The Science of Consciousness and the Methods of Ecumenical Science

NLIKE the social sciences, which count up to ten thousand religions that they seek to chart according to their differences, as do butterfly collectors, ecumenical science attempts to identify them according to their coherence and mutual relations. It does not propose a fixed and homogeneous conception of truth, but rather one that is dynamic and contextual, organized according to levels of consciousness and representation. In my book, *What is Orthodoxy?* published in French (Gallimard, 2013) and later in English (Angelico Press, 2018), I showed that, if one follows the main stages in the development of Western ecclesial historiography, spiritual rationality is expressed through four poles of human consciousness: the poles of law and justice on a horizontal plane, and the poles of glorification and memory on a vertical plane. The understanding of these four poles has produced in the history of philosophy two major conceptions of truth, as a mysterious self-revealing reality (*aletheia*, for the Greeks, means truth as the capacity of self-revelation) and as a divine and personal self-revelation (*emeth*, for Jews and Christians, means truth as faithfulness, constancy; a reality that can be trusted).[1]

As will be seen, this typology can be extended to the experiences of the two spiritual hemispheres of humanity: the monotheistic hemisphere, which prioritizes the truth-*emeth* (with its necessary interpersonal dimension),

---

[1] A. Arjakovsky, *Qu'est-ce que l'orthodoxie?* (Paris: Gallimard, 2013), 145–46; A. Arjakovsky, *What is Orthodoxy?* (New York: Angelico Press, 2018), 146–47.

and the cosmocentric hemisphere, which draws from the experience of the truth-*aletheia* (with special attention paid to meditation and awakening). We thus have a holographic vision of the religious experience articulated along two axes, vertical and horizontal. It is worth noting that a hologram contains three-dimensional information consisting of an image of interference between the waves coming from the photographed object and part of the same laser beam used to illuminate it. The details in the hologram are very small (in the micrometre range), yet the information from the whole scene reproduced is distributed over the entire surface of the hologram. A small part of a hologram can thus be used to reconstruct the entire image in a fractal manner.

This holistic view of conscience in three dimensions recognizes the various conceptions of truth that exist in their permanence and dynamics. As is well known, four major notions of truth have emerged throughout the history of philosophy: coherence, consensus, correspondence, and stability. Each of these four definitions of truth is magnetized by one of the four structures of spiritual consciousness. Coherence is linked to the pole of law; consensus to that of justice; glorification to correspondence; finally, memory to stability, both personal and institutional.

ELEMENTS OF THE ECUMENICAL SCIENCE OF CONSCIOUSNESS

The term consciousness implies, at the anthropological level, the capacity of people to understand a truth and to show wisdom made up of intelligence, will, memory, and virtue. A so-called unconscious person is someone who is incapable of acting, remembering, being responsible and understanding what they are experiencing. There are various degrees of awareness of reality on both a personal and a collective level. These degrees depend on a person's representations, personal culture, and levels of community belonging as a unique and connected being. They vary according to one's ability to relate to different levels of one's own personality, but also to personal realities beyond it. At a collective level, consciousness is made up of different strata, according to the relationships of proximity and empathy existing within a given group in time and space.

The paradigmatic levels of humanity's consciousness at the present time can be described as classical, modern, postmodern and spiritual. These levels are determined by a crystallization, often unconscious in individuals, of representations of God, Man and the world, within human communities connected by relationships that integrate and transcend the framework of languages, cultures, political and religious affiliations. *Oikoumene* is no longer understood in terms of inhabited land, and therefore of civilization inherited from Antiquity. It is no longer limited to the community of Christians turned towards the *eschaton* of the Kingdom. It is no longer understood as the space-time of the divinity ruling the world through the mediation of the emperor or the king, the patriarch or the pope, nor is it perceived as the domain of the absolute sovereignty of the nation-state and its general doctrine of human and citizen rights. The level of spiritual consciousness rests on an awareness of the spiritual life, understood in a personalistic, sapiential and ternary way, as the most authentic foundation of universality. These levels of consciousness can incorporate very different religious, and therefore cultic, traditions (polytheistic, theocentric, cosmocentric, theanthropic) which are the fruit of revealed traditions, but also of different representations of truth (representation of truth as correspondence, stability, consistency and consensus). They are shaped by multiple denominational (Catholic, Anglican, Lutheran, etc.) and religious (Judaic, Islamic, Buddhist, Hindu, etc.) traditions. These can be contested by very varied currents of conviction (atheist, agnostic, humanist, ideological). Each of the levels of consciousness gives rise to very different political, social or religious crystallizations. Thus, for example, the level of postmodern consciousness can give rise to different forms of populist government (some, as in Turkey, relying on the mobilizing power of Islam, others, as in Russia, relying on the resources of the Soviet victory) or to the emergence of different types of religious groupings (from dataism to transhumanism).

Alongside the levels of consciousness, there are different types of spiritual consciousness. These are determined by the different possible forms of subjectivation (which presupposes a degree of openness and willingness on the part of individuals) and objectivation (which enables human beings to produce shared knowledge). They are distinguished according to the syntheses operating between subjectivation and objectivation (separate, unified, excluding, inter-penetrated). These types of spiritual consciousness can generate various currents of thought (positivism, scientism, idealism, spiritualism, etc.) and religious practices (meditation, individual prayer, collective prayer, social engagement); they can be expressed in various ways at different levels of consciousness. Thus, the modern level of consciousness is characterized by a conception of truth as the product of theoretical rational intelligence. It has given rise to types of consciousness that have been termed confessional (Anglican, Reformed, Catholic, Orthodox, etc.). These different types of consciousness are in constant tension, which can lead to conflicts, dialogues, forms of co-existence, and syntheses. When syntheses occur, they can lead to changes in levels of consciousness.

The postmodern level of consciousness tends to bring the faithful together along new dividing lines that disrupt denominational patterns of consciousness. For example, the "defence of traditional values" or "commitment to the environment" goes far beyond Catholicism or Anglicanism. As they become more radical, influenced by the

postmodern spirit, they come to question faith-based institutions. However, as will become evident, this evolution
can also lead to a new level of consciousness, described as
spiritual, born of an awareness of the personal universal
character of faith/reason and the need to hold together
the different poles that structure it.

The types of spiritual consciousness are structured by
the magnetization between different aspects of the truth
captured by faith-reason: law/consistency, justice/consen-
sus, glory/correspondence, memory/faithfulness. These
aspects are presented in different ways within different
systems of cultural representation and religious traditions.
Thus, to take the case of the Christian community, we
can observe four types of representation of truth, as
worthy glorification and faithful memory, as right truth
and knowledge of justice. Within these systems of representation, we find different mythologies in relation to
paradigms that shape the different spiritual groups and
communities to which they belong. Paradigms, according
to Karl Polanyi and Thomas Kuhn, are scientific discov-
eries that are universally recognized, providing a group of
researchers for a given time period with typical problems
and solutions. These paradigms have the unique quality of
being in a position of dominance inside a given space-time,
of having an impact on how everyone in that space-time
views God, humanity, and the world. The objectification
of these paradigms, made possible by the evolution of
spiritual categories, allows them to be questioned, and, as
a result, allows levels of consciousness to evolve. The categories of consciousness existing within the different levels
of consciousness are expressed in various ways, depending
on the power of the paradigm, but also on the hold of
the political power over religious communities. The study
of these types and levels of consciousness can reveal the
decisive factors that explain the evolution, convergent
or divergent, of the different spiritual categories. It also

reveals the paradigm shifts that allow the movement from one level of consciousness to another. The Ipsos study on the six families of Catholics in France published by the newspaper *La Croix* in 2017[2] distinguishes, at the pole of glory, "the inspired," at the pole of law "the observant," at the pole of justice "the fraternal seasonal workers" as well as the "emancipated," and at the pole of memory "the cultural and festive," while the "conciliar" are at the intersection of these different poles.

Ecumenical science defines itself as the science of the universal, as well as the science of consciousness. It aims to understand what people, whether Christians or communists, mean by concepts such as "Catholicity" or "international," terms which have received different interpretations in history. It reveals the resonant relationship between the universality of intelligent faith and community self-awareness.

THE SPIRIT OF THE ECUMENICAL METHOD

For Régis Debray, "the only universalism that is not double-edged — in the moral order — would perhaps be that of method and not of doctrine."[3] The method he advocates is that of dialogue. It is part of the European tradition of maieutics, as defined by Socrates. Briefly, this consists of acknowledging one's own ignorance, and questioning the interlocutor, so as to encourage the emergence of ideas that are intuitive to him or her. In Plato's Theaetetus, Socrates states that his art of maieutics has the same general characteristics as that of midwives. The difference is that it is the souls and not the bodies that he is looking after in their labour of giving birth and recollection. Socrates is particularly conscious of the need to define the terms one uses in order to reach a consensus. The

---

[2] "Qui sont vraiment les catholiques de France?," www.lacroix.com (last accessed August 6, 2025).
[3] R. Debray, *Le Feu sacré* (Paris: Gallimard, 2003), 429.

method of dialogue therefore implies a sense of otherness
and listening. It does not seek to impose doctrine but
to empower and grow the interlocutor. Unlike a simple
debate, it always leads to a judgment that allows one
to determine the objective, and therefore social, truth of
its opinions. Philosophical hermeneutics is a path from
dialectic to dialogue and from dialogue to the conversion
of being. As we have seen above, ecumenical metaphysics,
based on dialogue, promotes respect for identities and
reciprocity as much as convergence and communion.[4] It
aims to understand God, the world and mankind through
the relationship of the I (we), the you and they.[5] Thus,
the hermeneutical method allows us to combine discourses
about God and the quests for Wisdom. The philosopher
Heinz Wismann reminded us of this ineffable link in his
book *Penser entre les langues* (*Thinking Between Languages*):

> I am for Pentecost, when the Apostles speak "in
> tongues." And while each one speaks in his own
> language each one carries the expressive authen-
> ticity that makes him a poet. And thanks to the
> Holy Spirit, they understand each other. This is
> the real utopia, "Between languages" is Pentecost.[6]

However, three brief but essential general remarks should
be made at the outset to clarify the specific understanding
of dialogue in ecumenical metaphysics.

Firstly, the notion of dialogue should not only be understood in the narrow sense of intellectual conversation. For
Gadamer, dialectics is the art of conducting a dialogue,
which implies the art of entering into conversation with

---

[4] My notion of dialogue was presented in a discussion with the
phenomenologist Michel Bitbol during a symposium at the Collège
des Bernardins organized with Nathalie Depraz in 2012: "Je, tu, il:
interférence entre philosophie et théologie — Collège des Bernardins," www.collegedesbernardins.fr (last accessed August 6, 2025).
[5] N. Depraz, ed., *Première, deuxième, troisième personne* (Bucharest:
Zeta Books, 2014).
[6] H. Wismann, *Penser entre les langues* (Paris: Albin Michel, 2012), 102.

oneself and seeking agreement with oneself. It is the art of thinking. "This means that it is the art of asking what exactly one means when one thinks or says something."[7] In this sense, as Gadamer reminds us, the hermeneutic approach always involves the translation of discourses.[8]

Secondly, the method of ecumenical metaphysics is to hold together the four levers of glorification and dialogue, asceticism and creativity. In this perspective, dialogue is not a privilege of the learned that could not be shared by the uneducated. For authentic dialogue is never self-sufficient. It is always oriented towards the horizon of the Kingdom. Spiritual traditions praise wise men more than learned men. In his letter to the Ephesians, the apostle Paul places humility, meekness and patience at the heart of the ecumenical method:

> As a prisoner for the Lord, then, I urge you to live a life worthy of the calling you have received. Be completely humble and gentle; be patient, bearing with one another in love. Make every effort to keep the unity of the Spirit through the bond of peace. (Eph 4:1–3)

For Christians, the emergence of unity is not the fruit of the Pharisees' morality, which demands that human decisions be measured against some ideal decision (Lk 18:9). Authentic friendship, that which unites God with humans and humans with each other, rests on the prayer of the publican and that of all those on the way who ask God to have mercy on them for their

---

[7] H. Gadamer, *La philosophie herméneutique* (Paris: PUF, 1996), 53.
[8] "Hermes was the messenger of the gods, charged with conveying to men the messages of the gods — and the Homeric descriptions often show that he literally fulfils what has been entrusted to him. But it is also often seen, especially in secular usage, that the work of the hermeneut is precisely to translate what has been spoken in a foreign or incomprehensible way into a language that can be understood by all. The work of translation therefore always enjoys a certain 'freedom.' It presupposes full understanding of the foreign language, but even more so of the true meaning of what has been uttered." Ibid., 85.

transgressions. Likewise, artistic creativity is decisive in the process of articulating and transmitting the beautiful and the true, the good and the just.

Thirdly, as Dagmar Heller,[9] a theologian of the German Evangelical Church and the former academic dean of the Bossey Ecumenical Institute, has wisely reminded us, the method of dialogue in ecumenical ternary metaphysics is not synonymous with consensualist unanimity, but rather with the ability to "exchange with different voices and words." For the theologians of the Radical Orthodoxy movement, courteous pluralism, characteristic of a certain tolerant and modern conscience, does not always serve the truth.[10] It can even dissolve it. Affirming that everything is compatible, or that everything is in everything, can make way for post-truth.[11]

In a collective work published in 1990 entitled *The Myth of a Pluralistic Theology of Religions*, the Anglican theologian and philosopher John Milbank criticized the modern view that only critical and ethical reason offers a form of universality that can unite all religions. In his view, the very concept of "religion" had to be grasped critically. For him, Christianity was not a "particular species" which belonged to a "larger genus" of religions. Rather, it should be considered as a new look at God, humanity and the world that reveals the reality and the diversity of the saving action of divine Wisdom in the world. The Church does not conceive of itself as part of a whole, with

---

[9] D. Heller, "Dia-Logos: Reflections on Different Forms of Inter-Christian Dialogue and Their Possibilities," in *Pathways for ecclesial dialogues in the Twenty-First Century, Revisiting Ecumenical Method*, ed. M. Chapman and M. Haar (London: Palgrave, MacMillan, 2016), 11–20.

[10] They take aim, in particular, at the following book: J. Hick and P. F. Knitter, eds., *The Myth of Christian Uniqueness* (Maryknoll, NY: Orbis Books/London, SCM, 1987).

[11] J. Milbank, "The end of dialogue," in *Christian Uniqueness Reconsidered: The Myth of a Pluralistic Theology of Religions*, ed. G. D'Costa (New York: Orbis Book, 1990), 174–91.

all due respect for the modern and tolerant State, but as the unique embodiment of the Triune God.

In another collective work entitled *Where is the Truth?* published in 2012, and devoted to a critique of the *Radical Orthodoxy* movement, the professor of Protestant theology at the University of Geneva, Shavique Keshavjee, criticized the approach of John Milbank. He considered it too critical of the theology of religious pluralism. However, the Swiss theologian agreed with Milbank that substantive discussions about truth should be at a metaphysical and thus theological level, and not only at the intermediate level of critical thought. He was also convinced that the "Trinitarian metaparadigm" testified to a love that respected the unity and diversity of the whole of reality. On the one hand, however, this conviction, according to him, should not "harden into arrogance."[12] On the other hand, theology had to be careful to avoid presenting itself as "confessional" in places, such as the university, where it is also expected to be self-critical. This was understood by John Milbank; the British philosopher has been involved in a number of philosophical and theological, inter-confessional and inter-religious dialogues over the last twenty years.[13] Through their remote dialogue, the two men thus converged towards a common position, namely that in-depth dialogues must occur at a level of thinking that is properly metaphysical and in a genuinely ecumenical spirit.

ASPECTS OF METHODS OF INTERRELIGIOUS DIALOGUE

Jacques Albert Cuttat (1909–1998), a Swiss diplomat and Catholic Christian, and Olivier Clément (1921–2009),

---

[12] S. Keshavjee, "OR et Théologie des religions," in *Où est la vérité? La théologie aux défis de la Radical Orthodoxy et de la déconstruction*, ed. H.-Ch. Askani et al. (Geneva: Labor et Fides, 2012), 95.

[13] See, in particular, the following dialogue in which I had the pleasure to participate: *Encounter Between Eastern Orthodoxy and Radical Orthodoxy*, ed. A. Pabst, C. Schneider (Farnham: Ashgate, 2009).

a French Orthodox theologian, were two leading advocates
of interreligious dialogue. Both agreed on the method
to be adopted and on the possible paths for a fruitful
encounter between the world's various religious traditions,
thanks in particular to the spirituality of Eastern Christianity. They both encouraged the hesychast method of
prayer, a word that means the ability to be silent, to find
inner peace, and ultimately, for the most experienced, to
see God. For them, the first position to take in dialogue
is a phenomenological suspension of judgment. The two
pitfalls of relativism and triumphalism are avoided in
this manner. There is no meta-religion superior to others,
as some esoteric streams believe. In this way, we guard
against the risks of Eastern syncretism and Western fanaticism. Olivier Clément expressed his concern over the attitude of dissociating Christ from the man Jesus. He also
invited us to recognize the violence of the first Islamic
conquests as fact, while learning to distinguish between
the Medinan Suras and the more peaceful and profound
ones of Mecca. It is also easier to understand certain
radical differences, for example between the Christian
understanding of the incarnation and that of the Hindu
avatara, or between Buddhist compassion and Christian
agape, as well as between the monotheistic vision of the
universe as creation with an autonomous history, and
the Asian conception of the universe as inevitable decay.
In this way we learn to better characterize the Eastern
hemisphere. Aware of the original identity of the human
being with the supra-personal and undifferentiated divine,
it seeks to reach the divine world through a phenomenon of the interiorization of consciousness. The Western
Hemisphere believes in the transcendence of the personal
God and the deification of man in God. To formulate
his view of truth's ecumenicity, Olivier Clément relied
on the principles of personhood and ternarity, as well as
the transcendence of duality:

> More profoundly, it is important to understand
> and spread ever more widely the mystery of the
> Uni-Trinity: the living God is so one that he
> carries within himself the reality, the pulsation of
> the other and, in the Spirit, in the Holy Breath,
> the overcoming of all duality: not by withdraw-
> ing into an impersonal unity, but by coincidence
> of absolute unity with absolute diversity. And so
> it is, at least in promise, in seed, in becoming,
> for humanity since man is in the image of God;
> total unity in Christ, total diversity under the
> flames of perpetual Pentecost.[14]

These two attitudes, of personal unity and non-duality,
are structural, and can neither be suppressed nor juxta-
posed. On the other hand, they can converge if they are
understood in a dynamic manner. Thus, in Japan, Buddhism has evolved in a theocentric way, from an ascetic
conception of religious practice to a belief in an eternal
Buddha (Amida). Conversely, in the Muslim world, an
anthropocentric phenomenon has occurred in some mystical currents. For the Persian Sufi Al Hallaj (c. 858–922),
the spiritual experience was especially marked by the sura
of the Qur'an according to which "Allah is closer to man
than his jugular vein" (Sura 50, 16). Islam can thus better
understand the mystery of kenosis, held by Christians, of
the voluntary humbling of God in evil and death in order
to triumph over it. For their part, Christians according to
Henry Corbin, can rediscover the meaning of uncondi-
tional hospitality in contact with high Muslim mysticism
and its angelology.

Thus, while taking care not to remove the existing antin-
omy between East and West, O. Clément and J.-A. Cuttat
thought it possible to hold the two spiritual hemispheres
together. For both East and West have the same perception of an intermediate, or imaginal world, that is to say

---

[14] O. Clément, *Rome autrement, Post scriptum* (Paris: Desclée de
Brouwer, 1997), 121–22.

the world of true imagination, between the visible and the invisible, where mind and body meet and unite in a common sphere, in dreams, in pilgrimages, sometimes in dance. The East can help the West to rediscover a culture of mindfulness, interiority, quietness and wonder, while the West can help the East open its eyes to the mystery of others, to stop seeing them as merely temporary commodities. A common journey is therefore possible on the path that unites the two sides of the experience of God as Wisdom and as Person. This expression is both taken from the Tao te Ching, which teaches that the Tao is the principle and the way to the true Name, and from the Gospel, where God incarnate presents himself as a way of harmony since he is "both truth and life." This expression, used by Christ to describe himself, means that truth can only be the fruit of a lived experience, while authentic life has meaning only in the discovery of truth through personal encounters.

THE INTEGRAL ECUMENICAL APPROACH

As a result of this journey through various approaches to interreligious and interconfessional dialogue, it is now possible to demonstrate the value of an integral approach that is both neo-holistic and transdisciplinary, as well as an ecumenical, personalist, sophiological, and ternary approach. This epistemology enables us to identify the "religious types" that cut across the many Christian confessions. These types of religion go beyond the boundaries of Christianity, and can act as the foundation for a true ecumenical epistemology of all religions.

We have presented the semantics of the notion of Orthodoxy to show both the reality of the commitment of Eastern Christians to the idea of faith-truth, but also the fact that this goes far beyond the framework of the Eastern Christian faith.[15] We have also highlighted the

---

[15] A. Arjakovsky, *Qu'est-ce que l'orthodoxie?* (Paris: Gallimard, 2013).

four types of religious mentality in the history of the Church: the zealots, the proselytes, the mystics, and the dissidents. The zealots can be associated with the pole of law, the dissenters with the pole of justice, the mystics with the pole of glorification, and the proselytes with that of memory. However, with the help of sociological surveys and interviews, it is also possible to observe intermediate types, for example proselytizers of justice (Pj) or the zealots of glorification (Zg). Moreover, if a group finds itself with more than 50% of people with spiritual values (S) and dissidents (D) then it can form a specific family (SD).

Thanks to this plural conception of religious identity, we can better "represent" with a certain coherence the diversity of the Jewish world, but also the Muslim world, or the worlds of Hinduism and Buddhism, as well as the dynamics of the groups and spiritual types that compose them. I want to emphasize that these are representations and currents in motion, not fixed categories or stable identities. Similarly, care must be taken not to identify established typologies with the realities on the ground. Distinctions between spiritual types according to their vision of the Church as the House of the Father (Justice), as the Body of Christ (Memory), as the Ark of Salvation (Law), or as the Temple of the Holy Spirit (Glorification), should be understood as typological generalizations. It is well known that within each Christian denomination, whether Lutheran, Catholic, Orthodox, or Pentecostal, there are different trends. The Mormons, for example, members of the Church of Jesus Christ of Latter-day Saints, founded in the United States in 1830, began as a denomination focused on the glorification of God. Over time, however, this denomination has become much more concerned with social justice. These representations are nevertheless useful for addressing the phenomenon of religious identities in a comprehensive and meta-confessional manner, as well as in their dynamics. They make it possible to trace the simultaneously homogeneous and heterogeneous, static and dynamic character of religious faith-knowledge.

As a result, it is necessary to add multitudes of nuances to the many holographic categories that are only provisional. However, first-century Judaism can be represented as a distinct entity, with the Essenes on the side of moral law and the Zelotes on the side of social justice, while the Pharisees are concerned with justice, and the Sadducees with the requirement of faithful memory. Similarly, there is a Wahhabi Islam that favours law over justice, and a Shi-ite Islam that, conversely, is concerned with social reform projects. There is a Sufi Islam, turned towards the pole of glorification, and corresponding to a mystical vision of the divine word made accessible through an initiation (*tariqa*), and a Sunni Islam that is more focused on its implementation on earth through Sharia law. The Sunni branch of Islam has several currents of interpretation of *Fiqh*, Islamic law. One can distinguish between: a current that is oriented towards the use of personal reason (the Hanafi school); a current characterized by the traditions (the Sunna) of the Prophet's Companions (the Maliki school); a current oriented towards the consensus of the whole community (the Shafi'i school); and finally a current that refuses all mediation and turns exclusively to the pole of the Qur'an (the Hanbali school, which itself developed in the Salafist tradition and then in Wahhabi Salafism, propagated by the Kingdom of Saudi Arabia). One can also make a distinction between a Vedic Hinduism (*Astika*) characterized by the law; a Hinduism magnetized by justice (*Nastika*), found notably in Buddhism and Jainism; a Sikh Hinduism structured around guru teachings; and a Hinduism of Bhakti, found notably in Tantric traditions. These mappings must be captured in a dynamic manner. For example, in Judaism, the pole of glorification must today be associated with the current of neo-Hasidism. Similarly, in Shi'ism, there is a strong esoteric current, concerned with angelology, as demonstrated by the Islamologist Henry Corbin (1903 – 1978) in *Le Paradoxe du monothéisme* (1981). However, these different mappings provide a certain overview at a given time. They suggest threats of division of the same type, but also possible paths to rapprochement, education and peace-building, both internal and external, which is the most important point for the most authentic religious traditions. Thus, the Buddhist Ken Wilber, in his book *The Religion of Tomorrow*, is aware of the value of such a holographic approach. His "integral spirituality" is nourished by the realization that Buddhism has an identity that is both dynamic (marked by four major Turnings centred on law, justice, moral perfection and concern for institutionalization through memory) and static (marked at all stages by the notion of awakening). For him, Buddhism is made up of a range of currents, from the Theraveda (pole of the law) to the Mahayana Buddhism of the Great Vehicle (pole of justice, represented by the bodhisattva), Zen Buddhism, the Japanese branch of Mahayana Buddhism (focused on meditation and perfection), to the Buddhism of memory and institution (represented by the tradition of the Dalai Lama, incarnation of Buddha).

Ken Wilber's interesting discovery, from the point of view of ecumenical metaphysics, since it is in line with the approach of Clement and Cuttat, is that a synthesis is possible between the two spiritual hemispheres, of the West and the East, through the meeting of the two anthropological structures of human spirituality situated at the intersection of the four poles of faith-truth, namely the growth of the consciousness of a community, from the archaic to the integral level, and the personal awakening, which rises from the struggle against the passions to mystical non-dual unification.

> Integral theory has discovered that humans actually have not one, but at least two major forms of growth and development. [...] These two

processes actually refer to two different axes of
growth in human beings. The first refers to what
are called structures of consciousness; the second
refers to what are called states of consciousness.
Thus, growing and awakening are crucial elements
of our overall spiritual development.[16]

As we shall see in the next chapter, in this great integral
history of human consciousness, the history of Christian
consciousness plays a nodal role. Indeed, since its origins,
the Church has sought to actualize the poles of catholicity and unity, of holiness and apostolicity. The Church
thought of itself, at first, as a new type of eschatological
community oriented towards the reception and realization
of the Kingdom of God on earth. Then, from the legalization of the Church by the imperial Edict of Milan in
313 to the great separations between Church and State, its
consciousness became more political. From the sixteenth
century onwards, this consciousness began to be thought
of in confessional terms and, from the nineteenth century,
it became interconfessional. Thus, ecclesiastical consciousness assumes a particular importance for the science of
consciousness. This kind of history makes it possible in
particular to account for the developments, distancing
and porosity between different religious communities, and,
within them, between different spiritual types. It values
the transforming agents (be they an emperor, a Saint, a
religious order, or a scientific discovery) who have made
possible, on the level of intra-ecclesial consciousness, the
passage from one level of consciousness to another.

In becoming ecumenical, the history of Christian consciousness participates in the elaboration of a third great
narrative of contemporary consciousness.

---

[16] K. Wilber, *The Religion of Tomorrow* (Boulder: Shambala, 2017),
67–68.

6

The Third Great Narrative of Contemporary Consciousness

THE history of ecumenical consciousness is part of the history of contemporary consciousness. It is neither the history of a universalist consciousness that suppresses differences, nor that of a consciousness of autonomy that legitimizes divisions. Ecumenical consciousness is the intuition, in living beings, of their common belonging to the same body, in different degrees of intensity. It ranges from the psychic consciousness of the smallest amoeba with tangential and radial[1] energy, to the spiritual consciousness of the human being with the capacity to know oneself through others, according to different representations of this otherness, from totemism to shamanism, from Judaism to Christianity, from Hinduism to Buddhism. This ecumenical consciousness is characterized by a form of knowledge that does not radically separate the hypothesis of concern from evidence. The historical awareness of the universal is a form of wisdom of life, that of the "included third," in constant tension between potential and actualization.[2]

Such a level of consciousness produces a new tense narrative of the history of interactions between the earth-system, men and their gods. This history, which began even before Herodotus's invention of the term *oikoumene*, goes beyond the sole framework of the Christian community and the limits of the chronology of Christianity. Conversely, this ecumenical consciousness cannot be

---

[1] P. Teilhard de Chardin, *Le phénomène humain* (Paris: Éd. du Seuil, 1955).
[2] S. Lupasco, *Les trois matières* (Paris: Julliard, 1970).

saturated by the horizon of the Anthropocene alone, as
suggested in a recent essay by historian François Hartog.
This conception of what would be the current regime
of historicity today remains profoundly modern, even
orphaned.[3] Yet the history of the world, whether it is
the civilization of the Mahabharata or the world of the
Bible, cannot be merely geological or climatic.

Chronological and anthropocenic consciousness only
makes sense in the perspective of a deeper and broader
consciousness, both sophiological and personalist. This
level of consciousness provides access to "real presence" by
bringing together created and uncreated temporality. In
this way, we emerge from "presentism," this consciousness
of being that F. Hartog characterizes as an obsession with
the present time, an inability to be part of a history by
virtue of not being able to get rid of the traces left in
the present by successive pasts.

On the other hand, we will focus our attention on
the level of consciousness that Christians have formed
about this history because of the power, at present time,
of the meta-narrative of Western Modernity. The Cana-
dian philosopher Charles Taylor was right to propose,
in *The Secular Age*, a vision of the spiritual, intellectual,
and civilizational history of Europe that combined a first
meta-narrative, championed by the British theologian
John Milbank — that of the misinterpretation of Christian revelation from the fourteenth century onwards (the
"ID" narrative, for Intellectual Deviation), with a second
meta-narrative — that of the permanent reformation of
thought about itself and of Christian spirituality that
affected Western consciousness in the modern age ("RMN"
for Reform Master Narrative).[4]

---

[3] F. Hartog, *Chronos. L'Occident aux prises avec le temps* (Paris:
Gallimard, 2020).
[4] The last sentence of his book *A Secular Age* is "We need both
ID and RMN to explain religion today." C. Taylor, *A Secular Age*
(Cambridge: The Belknap Press of Harvard Univ. Press, 2007), 776.

However, these two meta-narratives can be comple-
mented by a third great narrative, that of the Emergence
of Ecumenical Consciousness (EEC) in contemporary
consciousness. Faith-reason, as demonstrated by Vladimir
Soloviev and John Henry Newman, has its own history
in terms of ecumenical metaphysics. This third narrative
is no more anti-modern than post-modern, it is trans-
modern. It is neither theocentric, as in the Middle Ages,
nor anthropocentric, as in the modern era, nor techno-
centric, as in the postmodern era. If we may say so, this
third great narrative is *theanthropocosmic*, in the sense that
its portrayal of the evolution of ecumenical consciousness
draws together, within human consciousness, manifesta-
tions of cosmic consciousness and hierophanies of divine
consciousness. The person, as the emergent part of the
cosmic consciousness, as the interface between God and
his creation, is thus found at the heart of the process as
the referent third. Thus, by combining personalism, sophiology and ternary thought, this third narrative institutes
human consciousness open to the Spirit as the epistemological key to understanding the history of the world
and the ecclesial constitution of reality.

This ecumenical history of contemporary consciousness consequently makes it possible to put into perspective (without denying the contributions of the various
Churches to the coming of the Kingdom of God) the
confessional histories where these associate the conception of catholicity with the Catholic Church alone, the
representation of orthodoxy of faith with the Orthodox
Church alone, and the renewed sense of apostolicity with
the Churches of the Reformation alone. Unity, holiness,
catholicity and apostolicity are redefined as the modes of
expression of ecumenical consciousness. The orthodoxy
of faith, meanwhile, which judges conformity with the
Magisterium, Scripture and Tradition, is to be understood
as a truth in tension. It is no longer the property of an

institution, as demonstrated by Father Sergei Bulgakov or Pope Benedict XVI, but the revelation of its degrees of sanctity. For truth, in Christian theology, cannot belong to any one confession, since it is as much a gift, a phenomenon of self-revelation, as much as an expression of a relationship with the person of Christ.

This history of Christian ecumenical consciousness is all the more important now, since the collective consciousness contains a confessional mythology that cannot withstand historical scrutiny. Despite advances in ecumenical historiography, many media, newspapers, and magazines, even the most informed, continue to base their communication on a doxa from the confessional era. For example, it is frequently stated that the ecumenical movement began with the 1910 Edinburgh Conference, or at the very earliest with the creation of the YMCA (Young Men's Christian Association)[5] in London in 1844. This does not satisfy historians who regard Pentecost as the birth of a new kind of ecclesial community. It is claimed that the rupture between Christians of the East and West dates back to the fateful year 1054,[6] whereas there were ruptures before, and reconciliations after, this date.[7] One could also mention the oversight by contemporary churches of the saturated phenomenon of the ecumenical movement that was the Council of Florence in 1439.[8]

It goes without saying, however, that such a history of ecumenical consciousness, centered on the representation within the various symbolic worlds of what is the "universal"

---

[5] The ecumenical movement is only discussed in the ninth volume of the *Cambridge History of Christianity* in the section devoted to the twentieth century.

[6] L. Besmond de Senneville, "Les relations entre Moscou et Constantinople," *La Croix* (January 15, 2021), 14–15.

[7] See A. Arjakovsky, *What is Orthodoxy?* (Brooklyn, NY: Angelico Press, 2018).

[8] A. Arjakovsky, B. Hallensleben, eds., *Le concile de Florence, une relecture œcuménique* (Freiburg: Aschendorff, 2021).

Kingdom — in the spiritual, political and cosmic sense — is a call to a new trans-convictional and trans-disciplinary historiography on a global scale. To summarize briefly, the history of Christian ecumenical consciousness is marked by four major stages that have resulted in paradigms, presented above, representing the various meanings of the term *oikoumene*: the eschatological age; the political age; the confessional age; and finally, the interconfessional age, which is currently in crisis. As demonstrated by Father Gabriel Hashem, a Melchite theologian of Lebanese descent, this sophiological, and not only chronological, history of Christian consciousness (because it is both vertical and horizontal) is, in some ways, linked to four major wounds in the history of ecclesial consciousness: the wound of Christological disputes (in the fourth and fifth centuries); the wound of the mode of conception of ecclesial governance (eleventh to fifteenth centuries); the wound of the split between faith and reason (fifteenth to twentieth centuries); and the wound of different conceptions of universality, and therefore of international law and missionary activity (seventeenth to twentieth centuries).

From the birth of Jesus Christ to the legalization of the Church by Constantine in 313, history has been marked by an eschatological consciousness of God's Kingdom on earth. Since its inception, Christian consciousness has sought to comprehend the concept of universality through the lens of God's covenant with mankind, as symbolized in Genesis through the story of Noah's ark (Gn 9:13). In Deuteronomy, the word *Qahal* refers to the assembly of God's people on the day of the Law's promulgation through Moses on Sinai, which is also the day of the covenant's renewal (Ex 24:3–8). The Jewish community, acknowledging the failure of the monolithic and anthropocentric project of the Tower of Babel, pondered this universal covenant between God and humanity, made with Abraham and renewed with Moses. This was actualized with

the Ark of the Covenant and the Temple of Jerusalem as
the dwelling on earth of the Creator amongst His people.

The Christian community, for its part, has made the
Body of Christ the symbolic place par excellence for such
an encounter between God and humanity. Consequently,
the Nativity of Christ was introduced into the liturgical
calendar, and today represents one of the most significant feasts in the Christian consciousness. The Church is
where Christ is, and Christ is present each time in the
Eucharist, that is, in the act of the exchange of glories.
As stated by the Russian Orthodox theologian Father
Nicholas Afanasiev, "the unity of a local Church itself is
manifest in its one eucharistic assembly."[9] In John's Gospel,
concerning the temple in Jerusalem, Christ says to the
Jews: "Destroy this temple and in three days I will raise
it up" (Jn 2:19). Christ adds that such a personal understanding of the universal is only possible with reference
to the person of the divine Spirit. He explains to the
Samaritan woman that "a time is coming and has now
come when the true worshipers will worship the Father
in the Spirit and in truth, for they are the kind of worshipers the Father seeks. God is spirit, and his worshipers
must worship in the Spirit and in truth" (Jn 4:23).

This is why the *ekklesia* described by Luke in the book
of Acts is based on the event of Pentecost, namely the
impartation of the Spirit received from the Father by
the risen Christ to the first Christian community, in all
languages, to Jews and proselytes alike (Acts 2:11). Now
Pentecost took place on *Shavuot*, the feast of the giving
of the *Torah*, which also has a cosmic meaning, since
it marks the beginning of the harvest season. For both
Nicolas Afanasiev and the Catholic theologian Jean-Marie
Tillard, the *ekklesia* in Luke is thus not just a Greek word

---

[9] N. Afanassieff, *L'Église du Saint Esprit* (Paris: Éd. du Cerf, 1975),
29; N. Afanasiev, *The Church of the Holy Spirit* (Indiana: University
of Notre Dame, 2007), 33.

for an assembly of citizens. It takes on the meaning of a gathering of the people of God. It fulfills, in a universal way, beyond the Jewish people, the *Qahal* sealed at Sinai by the celebration of the Law.

> The Pentecostal community—the basic cell of the Church—thus appears as the manifestation, the *epiphaneia*, of the opening of the era of Salvation. This is so in the coming together, radically unbreakable, of three elements: the Spirit, the apostolic witness which centres on the Lord Jesus Christ, and the *communion* in which the human multitude and its diversity are contained within this unity and where the unity is expressed in the multitude and its diversity. These three elements belong to the very essence of the Church.[10]

The New Testament records many instances of division among Christians, but also examples of reconciliation, as was the case in Antioch when it came to welcoming non-Jews into the Church, and deciding whether or not they should be circumcised (Acts 15). Most certainly, the emergence of certain internal connectors in the life of the Church, which very quickly came to be referred to as ministries, facilitated such internal cohesion. In particular, it has been shown that the early Church, from the first century onwards, established a threefold structure for these ministries, with an episcopal college, a presbyteral college and a diaconal college. This organization prescribed the blossoming of different charisms or types of spirituality that had emerged during the first century and that St Paul echoes in his letters.

> Now there are varieties of gifts, but the same Spirit; and there are varieties of service, but the same Lord; and there are varieties of working,

---

[10] J.-M.-R. Tillard, *Église d'Églises. L'ecclésiologie de communion* (Paris, Éd. du Cerf, 1987), 22; J.-M.-R. Tillard, *Church of Churches: The Ecclesiology of Communion* (Collegeville, Minnesota: Liturgical Press, 1992), 8.

but it is the same God who inspires them all in
every one. To each is given the manifestation of
the Spirit for the common good. To one is given
through the Spirit the utterance of wisdom, and
to another the utterance of knowledge according to the same Spirit, to another faith by the
same Spirit, to another gifts of healing by the
one Spirit, to another the working of miracles,
to another prophecy, to another the ability to
distinguish between spirits, to another various
kinds of tongues, to another the interpretation
of tongues. All these are inspired by one and
the same Spirit, who apportions to each one
individually as he wills. (1 Cor 12:4–11)

Orthodoxy of faith was thus first conceived according to
the prism of worthy glorification, liturgical, eschatological
and sacramental. This is clearly seen in the ecclesiology
of the first Christians as recounted in the *Didache*, a text
written towards the beginning of the second century:

As this broken bread was scattered upon the
mountains and being gathered together became
one, so may your Church be gathered together
from the ends of the earth into your kingdom.
For yours is the glory and the power through
Jesus Christ unto ages of ages.[11]

The representation of the Kingdom of God on earth
became primarily political between 313 and 1453, when the
Byzantine Empire fell. The so-called ecumenical councils
of this period of ecclesial consciousness are a sign of the
political conception of the catholicity of the Church, even
if, because of the second meaning of ecumenism shared
by Eastern and Western Christians, they also reflect the
constantly updated validation by the ecclesial body of an
authentic participation in the life of the Spirit.

---

[11] "Le texte de la Didachè, ou enseignement des douze apôtres," in
Les Pères Apostoliques (Paris: Éd. du Cerf, 2001); *The Didache: The
Teaching of the Twelve Apostles to the Nations* (Michigan: Legacy
Icons, 2016), 8–9.

Each of the seven ecumenical councils, gathered from 325 to 787, retained today by the memory of the Orthodox Church (in the confessional sense of the term, since the Armenian Apostolic Church, for example, retains only the first three councils from 325 to 431) corresponds to seven interventions of the Emperor in the life of the Church in order to settle internal or external conflicts. Later in the West, from the eleventh century onward, the Gregorian reform contributed to the establishment of a papo-caesarist conception of sovereignty, leading to a centuries-long confrontation between popes and the new national states.

A new theology of politics, unimaginable a century earlier, was defined by Eusebius, bishop of Caesarea.[12] This he formulated in two speeches addressed to Emperor Constantine in the years 335 and 336 in Constantinople. For the German theologian Gerhard Podskalky, in Eusebius, "the immanent emperor has taken the place of Christ transcendent." Gradually, this semi-Arian vision was recognized as orthodox and imposed on the consciousness of Christians of the Empire:

> This only begotten Word of God reigns, from ages which had no beginning, to infinite and endless ages, the partner of His Father's kingdom. And [our emperor] ever beloved by him, who derives the source of imperial authority from above, and is strong in the power of his sacred title, has controlled the empire of the world for a long period of years. Again, that Preserver of the universe orders these heavens and earth, and the celestial kingdom, consistently with His Father's will. Even so our emperor whom he loves, by bringing those whom he rules on earth to the only begotten Word and Saviour renders them fit subjects of His kingdom. And as He who is the common Preserver of mankind, by His invisible and Divine power as the good shepherd,

---

[12] Eusèbe de Césarée, *La théologie politique de l'Empire chrétien. Louanges de Constantin* (*Triakontaétérikos*) (Paris: Éd. du Cerf, 2001).

drives far away from His flock, like savage beasts,
those apostate spirits which once flew through
the airy tracts above this earth, and fastened on
the souls of men; so this His friend, graced by
His heavenly favour with victory over all his foes,
subdues and chastens the open adversaries of the
truth in accordance with the usages of war. He
who is the pre-existent Word, the Preserver of
all things, imparts to His disciples the seeds of
true wisdom and salvation, and at once enlight-
ens and gives them understanding in the knowledge of His Father's kingdom. Our emperor, His
friend, acting as interpreter to the Word of God,
aims at recalling the whole human race to the
knowledge of God; proclaiming clearly in the
ears of all, and declaring with powerful voice
the laws of truth and godliness to all who dwell
on the earth.[13]

A century later, in the Church of the West, after the
sack of Rome, Augustine of Hippo (354–430) could not
help but notice the flaws in the theology of the semi-
Arian sovereignty. In 413, he began writing *The City of
God Against the Pagans*, in which he found it necessary
to make a radical distinction between the heavenly city
and the earthly city.

Accordingly, two cities have been formed by two
loves: the earthly by the love of self, even to
the contempt of God; the heavenly by the love
of God, even to the contempt of self. The former, in a word, glories in itself, the latter in the
Lord. For the one seeks glory from men; but the
greatest glory of the other is God, the witness of

---

[13] "Harangue à la louange de l'Empereur Constantin, Prononcée
en la trentième année de son règne par Eusèbe évêque de Césarée,"
Histoire de la vie de l'Empereur Constantin écrite par Eusèbe (Paris: D.
Foucault, 1686); Eusebius, "The Oration of Constantine Pronounced
on the Thirtieth Anniversary of his Reign by Eusebius, Bishop of
Caesarea," in *The Life of the Blessed Emperor Constantine, in Four
Books, from 306 to 337 A.D.* (London: S. Bagster and sons, 1845), 297.

conscience. The one lifts up its head in its own glory; the other says to its God, "Thou art my glory, and the lifter up of mine head." In the one, the princes and the nations it subdues are ruled by the love of ruling; in the other, the princes and the subjects serve one another in love, the latter obeying, while the former take thought for all. The one delights in its own strength, represented in the persons of its rulers; the other says to its God, "I will love Thee, O Lord, my strength."[14]

However, Augustine believed that God had created the fallen angels in order to serve the interests of the righteous, as he reveals in Book XI. Ecclesiastical authority could therefore use coercion to suppress sin. Similarly, he recognized that the use of coercion by temporal authorities was legitimate, on a temporary basis, while awaiting the second coming of Christ. The Church, for him, was the manifestation of the City of God on earth. As noted by the Catholic theologian William Cavanaugh, Augustine's vision continues to be based on an eschatological understanding that sees the State only as a fallen reality.[15] The difference between the two cities is temporal, not spatial. However, if the Church has the right to dispose of both swords, she can, taking into account the sinful nature of humanity, delegate part of her authority to the temporal power, as long as the latter aligns its right with that of divine justice. The new barbarian kingdoms, sometimes Arian, sometimes Christian, demanded no less. Augustine's representation of the "provisional Kingdom" made the advent of Christianity possible.

---

[14] Augustin, *La Cité de Dieu*, XIV, 28, 1, dans *Œuvres Complètes*, vol. XIII. Text revised by Jean-Baptiste Raulx, L. Guérin, et al. (Paris: C. Bertin, 1869). Augustine, *The City of God*, XIV, 28, in *The Works of Aurelius Augustine: The City of God*, ed. and trans. Marcus Dods (Edinburgh: T. & T. Clark, 1881), 47.
[15] W. Cavanaugh, "Church," *The Blackwell Companion to Political Theology*, ed. Peter Scott and William T. Cavanaugh (London: Blackwell, 2004), 398.

The confessional consciousness of the Church between 1453 and 1789, which can be defined as the moment of identification of one's own confession with the whole Church, was the result of a complex phenomenon. This identity-based and universalist vision of the Kingdom can be explained by a series of events: the victory of political Islam over Byzantine political theology; the failure of the reception of the Council of Florence; the promotion after the rupture of the Reformation in Central and Western Europe of the principle of "whose realm, his religion"; the consolidation of a clerical understanding of the governance of the Church; the growing separation between philosophy and theology, which gave rise to memorial-type affirmations; and the advent of a new form of missionary universalism, which was a source of profound divisions between different confessions that had become dependent on secular interests. The most common explanation is that religions entered the sixteenth and seventeenth centuries in a cycle of violence, requiring the intervention of secular power to bring them back to reason and place them under the control of a pacifying secular state. However, from a historical point of view, the concepts of a "religious war" and a "peace-making state" are problematic. In reality, the advent of confessional consciousness in the modern age was the result, in the first place, of the victory of a new theology of salvation, that of the modern state, over the papocaesarist and caesaropapist conceptions of classical consciousness. Indeed, we know that the so-called secular conception of sovereignty was theorized in France by Jean Bodin. In 1576, he published *The Six Books of the Commonwealth*, in which the sovereignty of the state is presented as unique, absolute, indivisible and untransferable. This was a clear reworking of the divine sovereignty of classical thought, but for the sake of secular power.

The theology of politics in Christianity, however, demonstrated to Renaissance men and women all of its limitations, most notably its inadequacy for evangelical theology. This is why Jean Bodin sought to develop a new model for encounters between different European religions. Between 1587 and 1593, he wrote the *Colloquium heptaplomeres de abditis rerum sublimium arcanis* or *Colloquium of the Seven About Secrets of the Sublime*.[16] This book presents a dialogue between seven scholars from three different religions (Judaism, Christianity, and Islam) about the merits of their respective religions. It ends with a most interesting conclusion in which the French jurisconsult offers to establish a balance between the different symbolic and religious realms through the recognition of a common compass for all. The latter is magnetized by the four poles of glorification (piety) and memory (mutual charity), law (goodness) and justice (Law).

However, the Enlightenment's deistic conception of divine universality prevailed over representations of the divine sovereignty of the men of the Renaissance.

From the French Revolution onwards, the secularization of the European courts was mostly anti-religious, and led either to the suppression of the autonomy of the Churches (as was the case in the Orthodox world and in most of the Churches born of the Lutheran Reformation), or their radical separation from the State (as in the Churches descended from Calvinism), or, finally, to a withdrawal into their own conception of the State, as was the case with the Roman Church, to the point of rejecting *en bloc* modern ideas of the Reformation.

However, from 1815 to 1995, this confessional and political consciousness, influenced by the romantic Renaissance, ascended three levels of ecclesiastical consciousness

---

[16] J. Bodin, *Colloque de sept savants de convictions différentes sur les secrets cachés des choses les plus élevées* (Paris: C. Defaut, 2011); Bodin, *Colloquium of the Seven About Secrets of the Sublime*, trans. Marion Leathers Kunz (University Park, PA: Pennsylvania State University Press, 2008).

one by one, to become progressively "interconfessional."

The so-called "unification" era lasted from 1815 to 1919, from the advent of the Holy Alliance to the collapse of the old international order. During this period of strong confessional paradigm dominance, the Catholic, Protestant, and Orthodox states united to block the way of the forces of secularization. However, during this period, the first awareness of the limits of a strictly confessional and political notion of the Church appeared, with Vladimir Soloviev (1853–1900), Johann Adam Möhler (1796–1838), John Henry Newman (1801–1890), and John Mott (1865–1955).

The "pan-institutional" period of religious consciousness spans the years 1920 to 1965. During this period, the ecumenical movement sought to structure itself, first through conferences, then through institutions, with the establishment of the World Council of Churches in Amsterdam in 1948 and the Secretariat for Christian Unity in Rome in 1960, both before the opening of the Second Vatican Council (1962–1965). With the decree *Unitatis Redintegratio*, promulgated on November 21, 1964, the Catholic Church affirms that the restoration of unity among all Christians is one of the principal concerns of the Council. It presents the ecumenical movement as an essential aspect of Christian life. The challenge was then to allow the renewed faith in the one, holy, catholic and apostolic Church to combine, in a creative way, the vertical axis of Faith and Order with the horizontal axis of Life and Work.

The subsequent period, from 1965 to 1995, can be characterized by a more "interdenominational" understanding of the Church, at least on a theological level, thanks particularly to the active involvement of the Catholic Church in the ecumenical movement. During these years of "peaceful coexistence," the ecumenical movement developed a critical stance toward ideologies, which contributed to its unity. The Church was no longer understood as the *Societas perfecta*, as in the time of the dominant confessional paradigm, but as the people of God and the Body of Christ. This period of doctrinal and social refocusing is sometimes referred to as the "Glorious Thirty of Theological Ecumenism," a period in which dozens of ecumenical, bilateral and multilateral agreements, such as the 1982 Lima convergence text "Baptism, Eucharist, and Ministry," were signed, and important texts were published, such as the papal encyclical *Ut Unum Sint* of Pope John Paul II (1995).

This period was followed, however, by a time of crisis. The upheavals in the world in the early 1990s, starting with the global extension of the neo-liberal paradigm, seized the interconfessional spirit of the ecumenical movement. The latter was associated by some Orthodox and Pentecostal Churches with a globalization that was disrespectful of confessional or regional identities. A rebalancing of power within ecumenical institutions was demanded by those currents, but also by churches concerned about a loss of identity. Furthermore, churches had largely forgotten to inform and involve the laity in the considerable upheavals in the representations of the Church made in the previous period. The result of these developments is twofold. On the one hand, from 1995 onwards, we have witnessed a radical reshaping of the ecclesial landscape, with the transition from the "inter-confessional" paradigm to the "transconfessional" or even "trans-religious" paradigm. This evolution can be seen as a very modern desire to reassure identities (political and/or religious) on one of the four poles of religious consciousness. New configurations have thus emerged across different denominational institutions: ecumenism of virtue, ecumenism of justice, ecumenism of tradition and reception, and spiritual ecumenism. On the other hand, we have seen a growing expression of radicalism in intellectual and spiritual matters in the last twenty years or so, with the main objective of reaffirming, sometimes violently, the power of religious consciousness, including its atheistic version, in relation to secular consciousness. This twofold evolution indicates that contemporary ecumenical awareness can only be reconciled and flourish at a new level of consciousness, that of ecumenical consciousness, which lies at the crossroads of the four poles of glorification and memory, law and justice.

However, the end of the Cold War was also a sign of the victory of the spiritual paradigm over capitalist and communist ideologies. This victory, prepared within certain ecclesial institutions such as the Conference of European Churches, gave a certain boldness to the churches. Thus, the major agreement on Justification between Catholics and Protestants, the issue that led to the Reformation in the sixteenth century, was signed in 1999. This agreement had been prepared and matured in the previous period. The enthusiastic atmosphere of the 1990s made the signing possible for most Catholic and Protestant Churches. In the following decades, new ecumenical syntheses appeared as well as unprecedented interreligious declarations, such as in 2019 between Pope Francis and Ahmed El-Tayeb, the Imam and Rector of Al-Azhar University in Egypt, with the "Declaration on Human Fraternity for World Peace and Common Coexistence." The in-depth questioning of interconfessional consciousness resulted in both a redevelopment of representations and identities as well as a spiritual renewal of ecumenical consciousness.

The history of ecumenical consciousness indicates that, spurred on by the vision of God's Kingdom on Earth, a new consciousness, both chaotic and progressive, has arisen over the centuries. According to the level of consciousness of divine-humanity, the desire for self-fulfillment can only be ultimately and presently fulfilled with and for others for the benefit of the common good. This vision does not reject, but rather integrates, the best of both modern consciousness (its sense of human dignity) and postmodern consciousness (its recognition of human finitude).

However, taken in isolation, the modern and postmodern levels of consciousness are a source of instability and violence. This is why the world is still able to develop in three different scenarios.

The present scenario, which tends to separate faith and reason, is one of the means by which the four types of consciousness within the four constellations of prayer, tradition, virtue, and justice are being strengthened, not only in the Christian world but also by other means in other religious and cultural worlds. The postmodern scenario, which eliminates or merges faith and reason, is characterized by a rise to the extremes of a conceptual and neutral universalism on the one hand and an irrational and senseless particularism on the other. Of course, these changes do not only affect churches and religions. The "ecumenical winter" is not a marginal phenomenon. It is both the counterpart and contemporary to "the crisis of globalization." The degree of consciousness accorded to the foundations and issues of ecumenical metaphysics is concerned with the entire political, social, and cultural life of the world's peoples. The UN Security Council will not be reformed for the sake of a new humanist right; the amount of plastic dumped into the oceans will not be reduced; free vaccines will not be given to every citizen on the planet without first considering the spiritual, epistemological and political framework that makes such developments possible. Conversely, the destinies of ecumenical consciousness are not reconfigured in an abstract way that is detached from the current urgencies of the contemporary world.

There is a third scenario, consistent with the gradual, albeit chaotic, emergence of an ecumenical consciousness of humanity over the course of at least three millennia.

It affirms the possibility of the coming of a spiritual civilization. An open rationality holds together the methods of analogy and fidelity, of coherence and consensus. This will depend on the level of faith held by different communities in the reality of a living God and the development of an ecumenical rationality by religious and convictional traditions. This resource of faith-reason enables humanity, on the one hand, to discern the inherent dignity of the human person and the created character of nature and, on the other hand, to participate in the action of Wisdom in the history of humanity and the cosmos.

From the perspective of an ecumenical metaphysics reordered to nature as creation and to the human being as microcosm and macrocosm, the role of each person becomes decisive in bringing about this appetite for Wisdom. Symbolic life cannot be decreed. It is found in its own inner self, and is experienced through a glance, or in the middle of a storm. The role of spiritual leaders is more important than ever in bringing forth, with wisdom and boldness, by word and deed, this faith capable of rationality, and this conceptuality open to whatever transcends it. The example of new convergences between religious and convictional traditions in peace-building is a real sign of hope in this respect.

7

New Ecumenical Practices

THE EXAMPLE OF PEACE-BUILDING

IT is quite clear that ecumenical metaphysics and the epistemology it entails disrupt many traditional representations of knowledge, and consequently many professional practices. From education to journalism, from artistic creativity to entrepreneurship, the advent of a new ecumenical and spiritual consciousness that transcends denominational, religious, and convictional affiliations is patently obvious.

The Muslim philosopher Abdennour Bidar, along with the movement of cultural creators and Alain Caillé with the convivialist movement, are pioneering a new, more open lifestyle and a new, more spiritual civilization.[1] A. Bidar advocates a new "weaver" identity that seeks to repair the torn fabric of the world, animated by a breath of spirituality and based on a new relationship with oneself, with others and with the environment:

> There are three main families of Weavers: the inner link, the social link and the ecological link. Their complementary commitment is fundamental because the "mother" of all the crises currently facing our human civilisation is the threat of a world being torn apart.[2]

This complementary commitment, however, is only possible if these weavers acknowledge Wisdom's transcendent rather than merely immanent dimension. Indeed, we have seen that Wisdom is the source of all links in different religious traditions. This source, which finds its origin in

---

[1] See www.convivialisme.org (last accessed August 7, 2025).

[2] A. Bidar, *Les Tisserands* (Paris: Les liens qui libèrent, 2016), 117.

the divine Spirit, is the only one capable of reconciling the "inner link" with the "outside link," whether social or ecological.

The convivialist school of thought is not hostile to such in-depth work. Alain Caillé and the authors of the Second Convivialist Manifesto have defined the five constitutive principles of this thought: principles of common naturality, common humanity, common sociality, legitimate individuation, and creative opposition. Everyone recognizes that the major religious systems have produced syntheses between these five principles. Because of the interdependence of these principles, they call for new dialogues between religious and agnostic thought. They thus join the efforts of contemporary ecumenical science in understanding contemporary consciousness and constructing new convergences.

> Convivialism is the name given to everything that in doctrines and wisdom, existing or past, secular or religious, contributes to the search for principles that allow human beings to compete without massacring each other in order to cooperate better: to advance us as human beings in full awareness of the finiteness of natural resources and in a shared concern for the care of the world. A philosophy of the art of living together, it is not a new doctrine that would replace others by claiming to cancel them or radically overcome them. It is the movement of their mutual questioning based on a sense of extreme urgency in the face of multiple threats to the future of humanity. It intends to retain the most precious principles enshrined in the doctrines and wisdom that were handed down to us.
>
> What is the most precious thing? And how can it be defined and understood? To these questions there is not and cannot — and must not — exist a single, unequivocal answer. It is up to each of us to find their particular answer. There is, however, a definitive criterion instructing

us as to what we can retain from each doctrine
in a perspective of universalization (or pluriver-
salization), taking into account both the threat
of possible disaster and the hope for a better
future. It is to be retained for sure from each
doctrine: what makes it possible to understand
how to control excess and conflict so that they do
not turn violent; what encourages cooperation;
and what opens the way to dialogue and the
confrontation of ideas within the framework of
an ethics of discussion.

These considerations are sufficient to draw the
general outlines of a universalizable doctrine, one
that can adequately wrestle with the emergencies
of the day, even though its concrete application
will necessarily be local and cyclical. Even if it is
obvious that there will be as many different, possibly conflicting variants of convivialism as there
are of Buddhism, Islam, Christianity, Judaism,
liberalism, socialism, communism, etc. (and, conversely, Buddhist, Islamic, liberal, socialist variants
of convivialism, etc.); if only because convivialism in no way claims to cancel these religions
or doctrines, at best, it can help to "transcend"
them (*aufheben*) — in other words, to consider
them in a synthetic perspective, by highlighting
their points of convergence to better imagine a
humanly sustainable future.[3]

This last sentence testifies to the fact that Hegelian
thinking is still very present in contemporary thought. It
also reveals a new quest for a religious synthesis capable
of bringing together, in truth and in justice, the principles
of unity and diversity. This is a valuable development,
since bridges between philosophers and theologians are
rare today.

---

[3] *Manifeste convivialiste, Pour un monde postnéolibéral* (Arles: Actes
Sud, 2020), 485–93; Convivialist International, "The Second Convivialist Manifesto: Towards a Post-Neoliberal World," *Civic Sociology*
1.1 (2020).

❧

Of the professions concerned by ecumenical consciousness, that of the diplomat and peace-builder is one of
the first to be affected. The shift from a conception
of sovereignty based on the identification of the state
with divine power to a representation of the state as
the guarantor of the sovereignty of the nation has had
important consequences in the twentieth century. The
rediscovery of the state in the twenty-first century, made
possible by such figures as John Milbank, Mireille Del-
mas Marty, or Pope Francis, as a public force for liberty,
equality, and fraternity in cooperation with the main
religious and convictional traditions, may also result in
a significant change in the law, and a shift from isolated
nation-states to pluri-national communities in solidarity. Over the past twenty years, significant progress has
already been made in the world in peace-building and
development through the United Nations Millennium
Goals, and now through the Sustainable Development
Goals (2015–2030). The UN estimates that the poverty
rate fell by 15% in 2015 compared to 1990. Improved
access to employment, food, sanitation and public health
(including the availability of vaccines) has added more
than a decade of average life expectancy to the world's
population.[4] However, disturbing statistics indicate that
violence has been on the increase all around the world,
even before the extension of the war in Ukraine in
2022. According to the British NGO Oxfam, 82% of the
global wealth generated in 2018 was captured by 1% of
the world's population, while the poorest half, 3.7 billion

---

[4] World Health Organization, Planetoscope — Statistics: World life
expectancy. "According to the World Health Organization, from 1950–
2011, life expectancy increased from 50–74 years in Latin America;
from 42–70 years in Asia; from 37–57 years in Africa," www.who.
int/data/gho/data/themes/mortality-and-global-health-estimates/
ghe-life-expectancy-and-healthy-life-expectancy.

people, received nothing.[5] One in three women world-wide has been a victim of physical or sexual violence. In 2018, military violence decreased in seventy-one countries, but increased in ninety-two others. More than seventy million people fled war, persecution or conflict. It is estimated that more than 700,000 people die each year as a result of war and physical violence. Military expenditure is constantly increasing in the world. In 2018, the United States spent $649 billion dollars, an increase of 43% compared to 2000, France spent $63bn (+15%), Russia $61.4bn (+239%), China $251.4bn (+423%).[6] The cost of the war in Iraq, which began in 2003, amounted to $330 billion in May 2006. In comparison, the annual budget of the World Council of Churches is 25 million euros.

It is obvious that violence is the result of processes that are located within the confines of the four poles of consciousness, memory and justice, law and glorification, and are the result of ignorance, poverty, victimizing mechanisms, and false religious representations. For this reason, it is necessary to offer peace-building education that builds on the accumulated doctrines and expertise of different religious traditions and secular institutions in matters of reflection, inter-religious dialogue and the definition of principles and methods that facilitate peace-building at the personal, social and international levels.[7]

THE RECONCILED DOCTRINE OF THE CHURCHES ON PEACE-BUILDING

In May 2011, an "Ecumenical Call for Just Peace" was signed in Kingstone, Jamaica, by over a thousand

---

[5] "More than 80% of the World's Wealth goes to the Richest 1%," *Le Figaro*, January 22, 2018.
[6] "SIPRI Military Expenditure Database; the 10 countries with the highest military expenditure in the world in 2020," businessinsider.fr (last accessed August 7, 2025).
[7] This presentation is a continuation of the course given at the University of Notre Dame on peace and ecumenical studies.

participants from a hundred member countries of the
Catholic, Protestant and Orthodox Churches.[8] The document asserts in particular that God is never the cause of
violence. This is why it is necessary to move away from a
theology of just war to a theology of just peace. Violence
is not natural; it has its source in pride, lies, fear and guilt.

> It [a commitment to Just Peace] requires moving
> from exclusive concepts of national security to
> safety for all. This includes a day-to-day respon-
> sibility to prevent, that is, to avoid violence at its
> root. Many practical aspects of the concept of
> Just Peace require discussion, discernment and
> elaboration. We continue to struggle with how
> innocent people can be protected from injustice,
> war and violence. In this light, we struggle with
> the concept of the "responsibility to protect" and
> its possible misuse.[9]

Consequently, the churches defend the right to consci-
entious objection and the right to asylum for those who
oppose and resist militarism and armed conflicts. They
raise their common voice to protect all humans who are
victims of discrimination and persecution on grounds of
political or religious intolerance. They also work actively
for peace education, which should be central to all school,
seminary and university curricula. In the final message of
the Ecumenical Peace Convocation, the signatories demonstrate their ability to bring together a whole range of
different yet complementary approaches to peace-building.

> We are unified in our aspiration that war should
> become illegal. Struggling for peace on earth we
> are confronted with our different contexts and
> histories. We realize that different churches and

---

[8] See World Council of Churches website: www.overcomingviolence.
org (last accessed August 7, 2025).
[9] Ibid., "Overcoming Violence," *Glory to God and Peace on Earth,
The Message of the International Ecumenical Peace Invocation*, at
http://www.overcomingviolence.org (last accessed August 7, 2025).

religions bring diverse perspectives to the path towards peace. Some among us begin from the standpoint of personal conversion and morality, the acceptance of God's peace in one's heart as the basis for peacemaking in family, community, economy, as well as in all the Earth and the world of nations. Some stress the need to focus first on mutual support and correction within the body of Christ if peace is to be realised. Some encourage the churches' commitment to broad social movements and the public witness of the church. Each approach has merit; they are not mutually exclusive. In fact they belong inseparably together. Even in our diversity we can speak with one voice.[10]

The unfortunate thing is that this approach has marginalized the entire Catholic tradition of the civilization of war, found in the doctrine of the misnamed "just war." As perfectly summarized in the *Compendium of the Social Doctrine of the Catholic Church*, "just war" implies a number of imperatives: the right to war (Latin: *ius ad bellum*) is reserved for a legitimate authority that must wage war for a just reason (starting with the principle of self-defense) and with correct intentions and objectives, while the right in war (Latin: *ius in bello*) imposes respect for several rules, including the proportionality of means as well as the protection of the civilian population and prisoners of war. A particular right is applicable to the final phase of an armed conflict, the *ius post bellum*, which includes peace treaties and their practical consequences. Unfortunately, Pope Francis seemed to have lost sight of this specifically Catholic approach to just war to the point of refusing to name Russia as the aggressor country in the war it is waging against Ukraine for a very long time, until January 2024. Only a meta-modern, properly ecumenical approach can find a synthesis between the classical and modern approaches to war.

---

[10] Ibid.

In the new differentiated consensus reached by the
Churches and Christian communities, peace/*shalom* is
built on a double axis.

On the vertical axis, we find two poles. At the apex,
peace is understood as a radiant presence that the faithful
receive from God. Peace is a gift offered by Jesus Christ,
yesterday and today, to a broken but loved world ("Peace
I leave with you; my peace I give to you," Jn 14:27). As
with the kingdom of heaven, it is like a mustard seed or a
treasure hidden in a field. At its core, however, peace can
only be achieved through memory work, the remembrance
that God is love, the reminder in human consciousness
of its own limitations. This allows for a gift in return, a
par-don ("through-gift"). This is how we must understand
Christ's exhortation to practice *preventive justice*.

> So when you are offering your gift at the altar,
> if you remember that your brother or sister has
> something against you, leave your gift there
> before the altar and go; first be reconciled to
> your brother or sister, and then come and offer
> your gift. Come to terms quickly with your
> accuser while you are on the way to court with
> him, or your accuser may hand you over to the
> judge, and the judge to the guard, and you will
> be thrown into prison. Truly I tell you, you will
> never get out until you have paid the last penny.
> (Matt 5:23–26)

On the horizontal axis, we find two other aspects of
peace, peace as a horizon of law and peace as a horizon
of justice. Indeed, peace can only radiate through each
person's own inner effort. At the time of his arrest in
Gethsemane, Christ asks Peter to put his sword back into
its sheath "for all who take the sword will perish by the
sword" (Mt 26:52). Similarly, only the establishment of
a just order can bring about peace. By sending his apostles on mission, Christ gives them the power to cast out
demons and heal the sick. He calls them to be "wise as

serpents and innocent as doves" (Mt 10:16). Christ adds: "I have not come to bring peace, but a sword" (Mt 10:34). A reading of this verse, based on the Kabbalah or on the teaching of the Pastoral Constitution Gaudium et Spes (78), shows that peace is not quietude and that it is built through an inner and ascetic struggle.[11] The "peace" referred to in this verse is understood in a secular way, as the apparent absence of conflict. While the "sword" here refers not to a tool of violence, but to the ability to reach the Yod, the Divine Spirit. According to the analysis of the Christian anthropologist Annick de Souzenelle, the warrior of peace, the nonviolent one, is the one who transforms the energies of his unfulfilled darkness into integrity.[12] Thus, according to the apostle Paul, it is appropriate to "overcome evil with good" (Romans 12:21). Peace-building is therefore the fruit of an individual and collective commitment to concord. This is achieved through the just glorification of God and the faithful memory of his covenant. It is also an inner struggle, both individual and collective, a taking upon oneself of external aggressions in order to transfigure evil through true proposals, attitudes of solidarity and the establishment of a just order. In the end, peace, like the Kingdom of God, is not a static state but a quality, a process of purification, of resistance to injustice, of sowing, of creation and of improvement.

THE COMMON PEACE-BUILDING PRINCIPLES OF RELIGIOUS TRADITIONS

For Eastern traditions, the attainment of inner peace is based on the practice of meditation, releasing negative energies and thoughts, and an effort of self-awareness. For Western traditions, it is attained through prayer, conceived

---

[11] A. de Souzenelle, *Résonances bibliques* (Paris: Albin Michel, 2001), 160.
[12] A. de Souzenelle, *Job sur le chemin de la lumière* (Paris, Albin Michel, 1999), 53.

as an inter-personal dialogue between God and man, but also between people themselves. These two approaches, according to the biologist and Anglican Christian Rupert Sheldrake, are not mutually exclusive.

> Meditation is like breathing in, directing the mind inwards; and prayer like breathing out, directing the mind outwards. Meditation involves a detachment from normal everyday concerns, with inward-directed consciousness.[13]

In his books *Science and Spiritual Practices* (Counterpoint, 2017) and *Ways to Go Beyond and Why They Work* (Hodder, 2019), the British scholar invites readers to acquire, in addition to the art of meditation and prayer, a sense of gratitude, an awareness of the universe and the joy of participation, through activities such as gardening or dancing. These benefit from the phenomenon of "morphic resonance," which refers to habit as a principle of formal organization of holarchical systems inherent in nature throughout time. To discover the life of the spirit, he invites readers to song, pilgrimage to holy places, fasting, sport, yoga, martial arts, etc. Sheldrake stresses the universal and trans-religious nature of these practices that reconnect soul, body and spirit. Through these exercises human beings learn to go beyond themselves, to become fully present with themselves and to experience forms of self-transcendence which in turn prepare for spiritual encounters. The pilgrimages that take place on Mount Athos and on the banks of the Ganges invite such encounters. Today, there are more than 300,000 annual visitors to Santiago de Compostela and six million pilgrims to Lourdes. Two million Muslims perform their Hajj to Mecca every year.

Even though there are significant differences amongst religious traditions, these spiritual exercises can have a complementary character. There are fundamental

---

[13] R. Sheldrake, *Science and Spiritual Practices* (Berkeley, CA: Counterpoint, 2017), 345.

metaphysical differences between Christianity and Buddhism. However, the Christian sense of the Holy Trinity, Father, Son and Holy Spirit, is not exclusive of the Hindu triad "*Sat-chit-ananda*" (Being-Consciousness-Bliss). Indeed, in the Christian context, theologians use the term "hypostasis" to designate the different Divine persons, whereas in Hinduism, one tends to speak of different self-consciousnesses. In both cases, intimately linked, one nonetheless discovers the origin of all being, the principle of creation, and the source of all authentic joy.

These immemorial practices can be performed by those who believe in heaven as well as by those who do not. They do not involve any form of proselytism. Above all, these exercises allow one to experience for oneself the depth of human consciousness, the radiant beauty of nature, the tenderness and warmth of divine energies. These practices make it possible to rediscover the sense of initiation dear to ancient societies. Rediscovering authentic initiation rituals by way of religious traditions allows one to experience, in a conscious and therefore guided way, that which souls unconsciously seek to accomplish. Singing in both the East and West allows one to experience the vibrations of the world. When properly taught, it enables people to rediscover themselves as a microcosm within which the complete harmony of the universe pulsates.

Ultimately, these spiritual exercises allow us to distance ourselves from the "hidden goddesses of materialism," starting with those who promise the omnipotence of knowledge. They offer an opportunity to recognize both God's presence in nature and nature's presence in God. Sheldrake shares this panentheistic vision with leading figures of twentieth-century thought, such as the Orthodox theologian Sergei Bulgakov and the Anglican mathematician Alfred North Whitehead. Rupert Sheldrake has conducted several studies of animal and human telepathy as well as of the phenomena of premonition, in which certain species anticipate earthquakes or tsunamis by their behavior. An awareness of these phenomena will eventually lead to the adoption of respectful and non-violent attitudes towards nature.

> The love that can flow through animals towards us, and from us towards them, may not just involve the animals' and our emotions but may be part of a greater flow of love to which we and animals are both connected.[14]

Similarly, a sense of gratitude can be a fulfilling learning experience for both atheists and believers. One progresses, in stages, from simple thanks for generous and free action, to collective social ceremonies, such as Thanksgiving in the United States. One can begin to experience the breath of the Spirit known as *ru'ach* to the Jews, *pneuma* to the Greeks, *chi* to the Chinese, and *prana* to the Indians, until the astonishing discovery that all reality can be appreciated as a free, supernatural and sublime gift. This learning of gratitude allows us to discover inner peace and also happiness:

> Study after study has shown that people who are habitually grateful are happier than those who are habitually ungrateful; they are less depressed, more satisfied with their lives, have more self-acceptance and have a greater sense of purpose in life. They are also more generous.[15]

ECUMENICAL METHODS OF PEACE-BUILDING

Sustainable peace is built primarily through the mobilization of committed and responsible people and civil societies capable of actively resisting violent situations without violence. This is all the more true as almost two-thirds of wars are related to identity-based conflicts

---

[14] R. Sheldrake, *Ways to Go Beyond and Why They Work* (Hodder and Stoughton, Kindle edition, 2019), 1080.
[15] Sheldrake, *Science and Spiritual Practices*, 826.

exploited by external powers. *Nonviolent action* (such as, on the negative side, protests, non-cooperation, product boycotts, disruptive action, or on the positive side, humanitarian aid distribution, petitions, awareness campaigns, competitive attitude modeling...) must be combined with *peace-building processes* (such as coalition building, training and communication with political activists, and finally negotiation with the relevant authorities) in order to achieve *conflict transformation* at a personal, cultural and structural level. This transformation must be aimed at the gradual eradication of violence, and at the development of a co-building dynamic for sustainable and just peace. A justification for such an approach can be found in the Kingston declaration:

> Nonviolent resistance is central to the Way of Just Peace. Well-organized and peaceful resistance is active, tenacious and effective — whether in the face of governmental oppression and abuse or business practices which exploit vulnerable communities and creation. Recognizing that the strength of the powerful depends on the obedience and compliance of citizens, of soldiers and, increasingly, of consumers, nonviolent strategies may include acts of civil disobedience and non-compliance.[16]

As a result, in recent decades, there has been a convergence of various religious traditions in support of a preventive peace alongside the single strategic peace held by modern states. Thus, for instance, American historians Nadine Bloch and Lisa Schirch have been influenced by the ideas and work of Mohandas Gandhi and Martin Luther King. The key point to remember from their various case studies is that agreements between inter-state

---

[16] http://www.overcomingviolence.org; *Just Peace Companion*, World Council of Churches, 2nd ed. (2012), par. 9 (2), https://www.oikoumene.org/resources/publications/just-peace-companion-second-edition (last accessed August 7, 2025).

elites that fail to involve or limit the participation of local populations affected by the roadmap for peace are unlikely to succeed. On the other hand, effective mobilizations are those that put people and civil societies at the center of the peace-building process, and succeed in bringing face to face representatives recognized as legitimate by key groups in these societies. Above all, a successful nonviolent campaign is one that can, on the one hand, denounce injustice, while, on the other hand, enter into dialogue with opponents to find alternative solutions to the problems that have been identified.

All the difficulty of the mass mobilization organized in Russia by the Foundation for Combating Corruption — now banned by the Kremlin — and led by Alexei Navalny is that the Russian government, despite the growing fragility of its legitimacy, refuses to engage in any discussion and only responds with arrests.[17] However, all that does is set up an even more chaotic situation, as is evident throughout the history of the Russian State. This is why, from the perspective of ecumenical science, the task of peace-building must first demonstrate the harmful nature of a false political theology of sovereignty for the Russian nation. It must also convince Russia's international partners, as did the International Olympic Committee at the 2021 Tokyo Summer Olympics, that it is mutually advantageous to deal with a nation rather than an individual state in some situations, even if doing so is more complicated in the short term, particularly when that nation violates international law and does not hesitate to dope its athletes.[18]

This objective of conflict transformation implies, first of all, a clear understanding of *the level of conflict in which*

---

[17] A. Arjakovsky, "Le Kremlin se remettra-t-il du film 'Un palais pour Poutine'?," *Ouest-France*, January 23, 2021.
[18] See my debate with the diplomat P. Vimont at the Normandy Peace Forum in October 2021 on this subject: www.normandiepourlapaix.fr/en (last accessed August 7, 2025).

one finds oneself. This allows us to move from an asymmetrical situation to a more balanced relationship between the competing powers and to promote *greater awareness of the causes and effects of conflict.* To achieve this, it is first necessary to learn to distinguish between people and problems. Successful resistance campaigns are "uncompromising on the problems but lenient on the actors."

The more united groups are around clear objectives, the more they are able to innovate tactically and the more they succeed. Cooperation between civil society actors is therefore essential for a successful resistance or civil disobedience movement. It is about facilitating the balanced distribution of power within different anger groups and about training activists and movements to communicate and govern together. But most importantly, it is about enabling a synergy between non-violent action and the skills of dialogue and peace-building. To achieve this, it is important to be aware of different possible situations. The Adam Curle diagram shows that the more a population is aware of a problem (abscissa), the more balanced the distribution of power within a society (ordinate), and the more likely it is to achieve a just and lasting peace.

STAGES OF CHANGE: ADAM CURLE

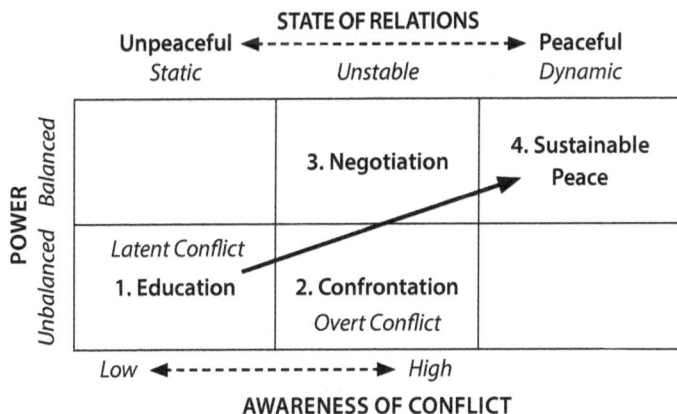

Based on Curle, 1971, as in Lederach, 1995

Certain tactics are therefore more or less adapted to different conflict situations. Thus, if a society is governed by a dictatorship and the population has a very low awareness of injustices due to a muzzling of the media (in this case, at the bottom left of the diagram), the work of building peace must first begin with uncovering latent conflicts through grassroots community organizing and raising awareness. Where there is open conflict (bottom middle of the diagram), it is necessary to inform wider population groups about the problem. One can take the example of the petition launched in France to inform the population of the State's inaction on energy transition and the need to bring it to justice for failing to meet its climate commitments.[19] On November 19, 2020, the French Council of State approved this action, and gave the French government three months to demonstrate that its policy was sufficient to meet its greenhouse gas reduction commitments.[20] In July 2021, the Council of State ordered the French State to spend ten million euros to improve air quality.

If the conflict is open and a power shift is possible (top to middle), dialogue and mediation work become more important than non-violent resistance. Conflict resolution includes

> any effort to increase cooperation between the parties in conflict and to deepen their relations by addressing the conditions that led to the conflict, by encouraging positive disposition and dissipating mistrust through reconciliation initiatives and through the setting up of institutions and processes through which the parties can interact.[21]

---

[19] www.arretsurimages.net; "The petition 'The Affair of the Century' crosses the million signatories mark," December 20, 2018, lavoix-dunord.fr (last accessed August 7, 2025).

[20] "Air pollution: the Council of State condemns the State to pay 10 million euros," August 4, 2021, conseil-etat.fr.

[21] Vatican, "Working for Reconciliation, a Caritas guide," *Caritas internationalis* (2001), XI.

It is not always easy to coordinate grassroots communities with the actions of diplomats, business leaders or generals. The role of religious leaders, intellectuals, MPs, senators and the media in this process is proving to be decisive. One might consider, for example, the role played by Émile Zola with his famous article "I accuse," published on January 13, 1898 in the newspaper *L'Aurore*, in allowing French society to shed its anti-Semitic prejudices and to push its army towards a greater sense of respect for the dignity of every human being, starting with Captain Dreyfus. More recently, it is worth mentioning the role of the Catholic Church in Colombia in organizing a mediation process that resulted in a peace agreement between the FARC/RAFC (Forces armées révolutionnaires de Colombie; Revolutionary Armed Forces of Colombia) and the government in 2016 after fifty-two years of armed conflict that claimed more than 160,000 lives and displaced 6.6 million people.[22]

It is also necessary to identify the interests of the parties in conflict — behind their public statements — as well as the deepest needs (or the most frequently unspoken legitimate reasons for a material, social, or cultural order) that are at the root of their conflicting positions. The Commission for Truth, Justice, and Reconciliation between Russia and Ukraine with the Mediation of the European Union, which we established in 2018, emphasized this point before releasing its forty proposals for peace.[23] Negotiations that focus on the desires/interests

---

[22] The historic peace agreement between Colombia and the FARC was signed (lemonde.fr, last accessed August 7, 2025) on September 26, 2016.

[23] "Projet de paix entre la Russie et l'Ukraine de la Commission Vérité, Justice et Réconciliation," Paris, December 2019, Note-Commission-VJR-FR-28.11.pdf (collegedesbernardins.fr); "What Peace Plan Between Russia and Ukraine? General Report of the Commission for Truth, Justice and Reconciliation between Russia and Ukraine with the Mediation of the European Union,"

of all parties (and not on public positions or the interests of a minority of the conflicting parties) have the advantage not only of focusing on the real interests at stake, but also of providing adversaries with possible emergency exits.

---

euromaidanpress.com: "Truth Justice, Reconciliation Commission: Russia/Ukraine/EU. 36 proposals for peace between Ukraine & Russia."

CONCLUSION

T is not only academics who can be strongly marked by the social doctrine of churches and the work for peace of the various religious institutions. Barack Obama, while still an Illinois senator, paid tribute in 2008 to an icon of peacebuilding in the twentieth century, the American pastor Martin Luther King. This tribute has a particularly topical resonance, as in 2020, the killing of African-American citizen George Floyd by a white police officer, Derek Chauvin, on May 25 in Minneapolis, sparked a global wave of protest against racism.

In his famous speech at the Ebenezer Baptist Church in Atlanta, in commemoration of Dr King on January 20, 2008, a holiday in the United States, he used the words of the Baptist minister: "Unity is the great need of the hour." In the midst of an economic, social, and moral crisis, Barack Obama, in a few words, updated this vital link between unity and peace.

> "Unity is the great need of the hour." Not because it sounds pleasant or because it makes us feel good, but because it's the only way we can overcome the essential deficit that exists in this country. I'm not talking about a budget deficit. I'm not talking about a trade deficit. I'm not talking about a deficit of good ideas or new plans. I'm talking about a moral deficit. I'm talking about an empathy deficit. I'm talking about an inability to recognize ourselves in one another; to understand that we are our brother's keeper; we are our sister's keeper; that, in the words of Dr. King, we are all tied together in a single garment of destiny.

The American president is not content to simply recall the memory of Martin Luther King, the metaphysical and moral link that unites unity and peace. He calls on his fellow citizens to show compassion by helping them to open their eyes to reality.

> We have an empathy deficit when we're still send-
> ing our children down corridors of shame, schools
> in the forgotten corners of America where the
> color of your skin still affects the content of your
> education. We have a deficit when CEOs are
> making more in ten minutes than some workers
> make in ten months; when families lose their
> homes so that lenders make a profit; when moth-
> ers can't afford a doctor when their children get
> sick. [...] And we have a deficit when it takes
> a breach in our levees to reveal a breach in our
> compassion; when it takes a terrible storm to
> reveal the hungry that God calls on us to feed;
> the sick He calls on us to care for; the least of
> these He commands that we treat as our own. So
> we have a deficit to close. We have walls, "barriers
> to justice and equality" that must come down.
> And to do this, we know that unity is the great
> need of this hour.[1]

President Obama invokes categories transcending the legal and secular order in order to encourage everyone to discern.[2] Only an ecumenical worldview allows a country to become a nation. Joseph Biden understood this, twelve years later, when the political and social situation in the United States had worsened considerably following Donald Trump's tenure. In his inaugural address on January 20, 2021, the new American president spoke of the spiritual link between unity and peace:

> And now, a rise in political extremism, white
> supremacy, domestic terrorism that we must

---

[1] See www.scripts.mit.edu, dated January 20, 2008: https://scripts.mit.edu/~birge/blog/obamas-speech-at-eben (last accessed August 7, 2025).

[2] In this way B. Obama embodies what the philosopher J.-M. Ferry recommended in his book *Les lumières de la religion*. J.-M. Ferry, *Les lumières de la religion. Entretien avec Élodie Maurot. Les religions dans l'espace public* (Paris: Bayard, 2003).

confront and we will defeat. To overcome these
challenges — to restore the soul and to secure
the future of America — requires more than
words. It requires that most elusive of things
in a democracy: Unity.[3]

It is remarkable that some contemporary politicians
are sensitive to a spiritual approach to peace-building and
understand the importance of reconnecting morality and
political science. The fact remains, however, that state
spending on weapons has never been as high as it is
today: two thousand billion dollars in 2020, according
to SIPRI.[4] Let us also remember the astronomical sums
spent by the United States in Afghanistan over a period
of twenty years: two trillion dollars or three hundred
million euros per day between 2001 and 2021...[5]

This is why the time has probably come to make more
deeply known the social doctrine of the churches on peace
and the spiritual resources of the different religious traditions. This is to raise awareness and to establish genuine
peace within the nations of the world. As I suggested
in 2013 in my essay *For a Personalist Democracy*, it has
become urgent to balance the concept of strategic peace
with that of preventive peace.[6] Such a vision is rooted
in a deeper understanding of peace. Pope Francis speaks
of an "architecture of peace, where each individual can
act as an effective leaven by the way he or she lives each
day." However, again, the implementation of such a vision,
which is actively supported by the Kroc Institute at the

---

[3] "Inaugural Address by President Joseph R. Biden, Jr.," January, 20,
2021, https://www.whitehouse.gov/briefing-room/speeches-remarks/
2021/01/20/inaugural-address-by-president-joseph-r-biden-jr/.
[4] "2,000 billion in global military spending in 2020," *La Croix*,
April 29, 2021.
[5] "Afghanistan: What has the conflict cost the US and its allies?,"
BBC News, September 3, 2021.
[6] A. Arjakovsky, *Pour une démocratie personnaliste* (Paris: Lethielleux, 2013).

University of Notre Dame,[7] for example, will only be possible if politicians and above all public opinion make the effort to take ecumenical metaphysics seriously.

Ecumenical metaphysics alone recognizes the full implications of the fact that budgets are always moral documents.[8] Ecumenical metaphysics, in particular, allows for a balance between distributive truth-justice, which consists of granting each person his due share according to the ideal of equality, and appreciative truth-justice, which consists of considering, according to the ideal of freedom, the intention of actions rather than their results alone. It also combines the horizon of substitutive truth-justice, which represents the effort to come to terms with social tensions in the name of the ideal of fraternity, with creative truth-justice, which consists of regulating violations of collectively established rules through criminal law in a personalistic manner, in the name of the ideal of practical wisdom. In this way, we succeed in promoting a law in tension, adapted to situations, resolutely oriented towards the common good, and implying the responsibility of each individual.

As the Belgian diplomat Thomas Antoine says, such work is not merely theoretical; it must be put into daily practice in the drafting of the smallest diplomatic telegram or in welcoming the most insignificant foreign delegation: "The diplomat must have a listening heart. He is both rational and relational. The listening heart, 'leb shomea,' according to Solomon (1 Kings 3:9), forges the man of peace. His truth is practical, his speech performative, his vision effective." To be performative, language must be inhabited, convincing rather than conquering. Without ethics, it is only a dehumanized messenger, a robot,

---

[7] Kroc Institute for International Peace Studies // University of Notre Dame (nd.edu) (last accessed August 7, 2025).

[8] A. Arjakovsky, *Qu'est-ce que la science morale et politique?* (Paris: Cerf, 2025).

echoing the discourses justifying power relations, without faith, without hope, and without charity.

This diplomacy of the Spirit, founded in the sixteenth century by Ignatius of Loyola on the examination of conscience, is therefore based on four pillars:

℩ benevolence, motivated by the diplomat's desire to defend the common good, that is, social cohesion, justice, and peace;

℩ lucidity, which requires introspection, examination of conscience, and regular verification of the results achieved;

℩ flexibility of mind without losing sight of the objective, or the ability to adapt to different situations in cultures, spaces, times, and customs;

℩ finally, fortitude, courage, heroism, and self-improvement are the capacities to bring out the best in each person, which leads to pride in having shared the same ordeal, in having risen to the same challenge, in having given greater meaning to one's life.

This rehabilitation of the diplomacy of the Spirit in the face of the pseudo-realism of contemporary geopolitics could yield a number of fruits.

ABOUT THE AUTHOR

ANTOINE ARJAKOVSKY founded the Institute of Ecumenical Studies in Lviv at the Ukrainian Catholic University in 2004. He directed this institute for ten years and was involved in the international ecumenical movement, particularly the Conference of European Churches and the Faith and Order Commission within the World Council of Churches. He also founded the Ecumenical Social Weeks and the Christian Academic Society in Ukraine. Author of some twenty books on philosophy, theology, political science, and history, he directed for five years the Association of Christian Philosophers in France. He is currently a research director at the Collège des Bernardins in Paris and administrator of the Platform for European Memory and Conscience, based in Prague.

www.ingramcontent.com/pod-product-compliance
Lightning Source LLC
Chambersburg PA
CBHW021147090426
42740CB00008B/981

* 9 7 9 8 8 9 2 8 0 1 5 4 6 *

9 798892 801546